you can RENEW this item from
home by visiting our Website at
www.woodbridge.lioninc.org or by
calling (203) 389-3433

Read On . . . Romance

Read On . . . Romance

Reading Lists for Every Taste

C. L. Quillen and Ilene N. Lefkowitz

Read On Series
Barry Trott, Series Editor

AN IMPRINT OF ABC-CLIO, LLC
Santa Barbara, California • Denver, Colorado • Oxford, England

Library of Congress Cataloging-in-Publication Data

Quillen, C. L.
　Read on . . . romance : reading lists for every taste / C.L. Quillen and Ilene N. Lefkowitz.
　　pages cm — (Read on series)
　Includes bibliographical references and index.
　ISBN 978-1-61069-400-1 (paperback) — ISBN 978-1-61069-401-8 (ebook)
1. Love stories—Bibliography.　2. Love stories—History and criticism.
3. Reading interests.　4. Books and reading.　I. Lefkowitz, Ilene N.
II. Title.　III. Title: Romance : reading lists for every taste.
　Z1231.L68Q55　2014
　[PN3448.L67]
　016.80883'85—dc23　　　2014005515

ISBN: 978-1-61069-400-1
EISBN: 978-1-61069-401-8

18　17　16　15　14　　1　2　3　4　5

This book is also available on the World Wide Web as an eBook.
Visit www.abc-clio.com for details.

Libraries Unlimited
An Imprint of ABC-CLIO, LLC

ABC-CLIO, LLC
130 Cremona Drive, P.O. Box 1911
Santa Barbara, California 93116-1911

This book is printed on acid-free paper (∞)

Manufactured in the United States of America

To Ray—Your armor might be a little tarnished and I'm no fairy princess, but I think we're living our own mostly happy ever after. Loves you!

To Mom—Thanks for everything, but mostly for inspiring in me a love of reading.

To Ilene—I couldn't have done it without you.

To romance readers and the librarians who support them, we hope you never run out of something great to read.

—C. L.

To H & P for being incredibly understanding throughout this process and for being the best cheerleaders I could ask for.

To Mom—You always said that I would write a book. Thank you for never losing faith in me.

To Jeff for everything. Loce you.

To C.L. for asking me to be a part of this amazing adventure. It has been crazy, stressful, and more fun than I could have ever imagined. Thank you.

—Ilene

Contents

Series Foreword

Welcome to Libraries Unlimited's Read On series of fiction and nonfiction genre guides for readers' advisors and for readers. The Read On series introduces readers and those who work with them to new ways of looking at books, genres, and reading interests.

Over the past decade, readers' advisory services have become vital in public libraries. A quick glance at the schedule of any library conference at the state or national level will reveal a wealth of programs on various aspects of connecting readers to books they will enjoy. Working with unfamiliar genres or types of reading can be a challenge, particularly for those new to the field. Equally, readers may find it a bit overwhelming to look for books outside their favorite authors and preferred reading interests. The titles in the Read On series offer you a new way to approach reading:

- they introduce you a broad sampling of materials available in a given genre;
- they offer you new directions to explore in a genre—through appeal features and unconventional topics;
- they help readers' advisors better understand and navigate genres with which they are less familiar; and
- they provide reading lists that you can use to create quick displays, include on your library websites and in the library newsletter, or to hand out to readers.

The lists in the Read On series are arranged in sections based on appeal characteristics—story, character, setting, and language (as described in Joyce Saricks's *Reader's Advisory Services in the Public Library,* 3d ed., ALA Editions, 2005), with a fifth section on mood. These are hidden elements of a book that attract readers. Remember that a book can have multiple appeal factors, and sometimes readers are drawn to a particular book for several factors, while other times for only one. In the Read On lists, titles are placed according to their primary appeal characteristics, and then put into a list that reflects common reading interests. So if you are working with a reader who loves fantasy that features quests for magical objects or a reader who is interested in memoirs with a strong sense of place, you will be able to find a list of titles whose main appeal centers around this search. Each list indicates a title that is an especially good starting place for readers, an exemplar of that appeal characteristic.

Story is perhaps the most basic appeal characteristic. It relates to the plot of the book—what are the elements of the tale? Is the emphasis more on the people or the situations? Is the story action focused or more interior? Is it funny? Scary?

Many readers are drawn to the books they love by the characters. The character appeal reflects such aspects as whether there are lots of characters or only a single main character; are the characters easily recognizable types? Do the characters grow and change over the course of the story? What are the characters' occupations?

Setting covers a range of elements that might appeal to readers. What is the time period or geographic locale of the tale? How much does the author describe the surroundings of the story? Does the reader feel as though he or she is "there," when reading the book? Are there special features such as the monastic location of Ellis Peters's <u>Brother Cadfael Mysteries</u> or the small-town setting of Jan Karon's <u>Mitford</u> series?

Although not traditionally considered appeal characteristic, mood is important to readers as well. It relates to how the author uses the tools of narrative—language, pacing, story, and character—to create a feeling for the work. Mood can be difficult to quantify because the reader brings his or her own feelings to the story as well. Mood really asks, how does the book make the reader feel? Creepy? Refreshed? Joyful? Sad?

Finally, the language appeal brings together titles where the author's writing style draws the reader. This can be anything from a lyrical prose style with lots of flourishes to a spare use of language à la Hemingway. Humor, snappy dialog, word-play, recipes, and other language elements all have the potential to attract readers.

Dig into these lists. Use them to find new titles and authors in a genre that you love, or as a guide to expand your knowledge of a new type of writing. . . . Above all, read, enjoy, and remember—never apologize for your reading tastes!

—Barry Trott
Series Editor

Introduction

Readers understand that the books celebrate female power. In the romance novel, the woman always wins. With courage, intelligence and gentleness she brings the most dangerous creature on the earth, the human male, to his knees.

—Jayne Ann Krentz

Romance gets a bad rap. Despite their popularity, many people still describe romances as bodice rippers, trashy reading, and porn for women. There is a belief that because they have a happy ending they are formulaic, with only the characters' names and occupations changing from book to book. But romance offers hope to readers. They see the characters struggle, develop problem-solving skills, and work to improve their relationships.

One of the reasons that Romance is so popular is that books in this genre provide readers with an emotional connection to the characters. Readers get to know the people who live in these books, learning their likes and dislikes, personal characteristics, friends and family while they journey with the hero and heroine through their conflicts to a satisfying and happy conclusion.

The Appeal of Romance

Romance novels appeal to readers young and old. Readers cherish the connections that romance novels allow them to make. Series readers will tell you that they look forward to the next book in a series because it is like visiting old friends. While the main characters may be someone new to the book's universe, you can always count on characters from former books popping up here and there. In today's chaotic world, it is refreshing to be able to have something to count on. With the wide spectrum of subgenres and level of intimacy, there is something for every type of romance reader.

Organization

This book is divided into five categories based on appeal factors: Story, Character, Mood, Language, and Setting. Each chapter is divided further into lists, which have six to ten recommended titles, which have been annotated to highlight their appeal. These lists can be used to create displays, as the starting point for more in-depth annotated book lists, or in print and Web-based library publications. We have provided brief, engaging annotations with series information, where applicable, and indicated our recommended choices for readers new to the world of romance novels. YA titles and award winners are noted.

How to Use This Book

This book is intended for anyone who loves the genre—Librarians, Booksellers, General Readers. The lists that we've chosen are not meant to be comprehensive. For each category, we could have created many other lists, and for each list, dozens of other books could have been chosen. We selected books that we thought would have wide appeal based on our own personal knowledge and tastes and by reading lots of book reviews, both professional and by general readers.

The lists are sorted alphabetically and for each list, we've selected one book as a place to start.

Symbols Used in Annotations

 RITA Award Winner
 Young Adult Book
 Start Here

Chapter One

Story

Many readers enjoy reading romance because it offers them a great story with the guarantee of a happy ending. They know the main characters will fall in love, but their interest is in the journey. How do they get from where they are at the beginning, through the issues they encounter, and come out the other side a couple? Books in the Story section focus on the plot; they are driven by the intricacies, the twists, the turns, and the way it all comes together.

You Were Always on My Mind

Ever wonder about the one who got away? These couples have another chance for love. Can they make it work the second time around?

Beckett, Macy.
Sultry with a Twist. 2012. Sourcebooks Casablanca. ISBN 9781402270369. 314pp.
Mae-June July Augustine left Sultry Springs, Texas, nine years ago vowing never to return. While in college, she discovered that she really loved mixing drinks, a career choice that alienated her from her Christian fundamentalist grandmother, Prudence. June is on the verge of opening the hottest martini bar in Austin, but first she must clear up a bogus warrant for indecent exposure that she didn't know she had from the time she and her high school sweetheart, Luke Gallagher, got caught skinny dipping. To do that she must return to Sultry and do a month of community service beside Luke. After a stint in the military, he returns to his hometown and runs a construction company. Luke doesn't believe in love—his mother abandoned him when he was 12 and he's divorced.

Luke and June are vulnerable and insecure. June risks her heart, but will she be able to teach Luke to love? This is a clever, well-written debut with plenty of small-town Texas charm and witty dialogue. *Sultry with a Twist* kicks off the <u>Sultry Springs</u> series.

Bradley, Celeste and Donovan, Susan.
A Courtesan's Guide to Getting Your Man. 2011. St. Martin's Press. ISBN 97803 12532567. 384pp.

Things are not going well for mousy museum curator Piper Chase-Pierpont—she hasn't had a relationship in years, her lips are stained blue, and she may lose her job. Piper is putting together a display about Ophelia Harrington, a woman known for her abolitionist work during the Civil War. While going through Ophelia's trunk, she finds Ophelia's diary and learns that prior to coming to America, Ophelia was Regency England's most infamous courtesan, Blackbird. Piper reads Ophelia's diaries, and when Mick Malloy, the guy Piper has never forgotten, reenters her life, she is empowered to make a change. Piper makes herself over as a confident, sexy woman. Bradley and Donovan prove that two love stories are better than one. Transitioning easily between the past and the present, this sizzling collaboration will appeal to readers of both contemporary and historical romance.

English, Christy.
Love on a Midsummer Night. 2013. Sourcebooks. ISBN 9781402270482. 314pp.

Ten years ago, Arabella Darlington was forced to marry the elderly Duke of Hawthorne instead of her true love, Raymond Olivier, Earl of Pembroke. When her husband dies, his nephew tries to force her to marry him. Arabella goes to Pembroke and asks for his help. Pembroke has become one of the most notorious womanizers in all of London after he was betrayed by Arabella but he is still attracted to her. Arabella and Pembroke run away to his country estate. English's Regency retelling of *A Midsummer Night's Dream* is enchanting. (<u>Shakespeare in Love</u>, #2)

Gibson, Rachel. ♛
▶ *Not Another Bad Date*. 2008. Avon. ISBN 9780061178047 384pp.

After yet another bad date (she'd had so many she was beginning to think she'd been cursed), fantasy author Adele Harris has sworn off men. She moves back to Cedar Creek, Texas, to help her sister, Sherilyn after her marriage hits the skids. Adele has barely settled in when Sherilyn ends up in the hospital on bed rest, leaving Adele in charge of her teenage niece. Picking up Kendra from her best friend's house, she is shocked to find that the father of Kendra's BFF is Zach Zemaitis, the football player she loved and lost to a mean girl in college. Zach retired from the NFL and is now the high school football coach. He was widowed three years ago when his wife (who did, in fact, curse Adele) was hit by a garbage truck. The sparks between them are still there, but is Zach the one or will he be just another bad date? Compelling family relationships and a touch of the paranormal elevate this light-hearted romance. This is the final book in Gibson's Sex, Lies, and Online Dating series, about four writer friends who each get their own book.

Higgins, Kristan.
My One and Only. 2011. HQN Books. ISBN 9780373775576. 384pp.

Higgins charms with a sweet romantic comedy about true love and second chances. Divorce attorney Harper James was once married to the love of her life, Nick Lowery, but their marriage imploded after less than a year. She has been dating Dennis for the past few years, and while it isn't the love of a lifetime, they are comfortable together. Harper has just proposed, but before Dennis can give her an answer, her step-sister Willa calls to say she is getting married and wants Harper to be there. Harper has concerns; not only will this be Willa's third wedding, but she is marrying Nick's younger brother. When Harper is stranded in Montana after the wedding, Nick offers to drive her across the country. An emotional journey of self-discovery follows as they come to terms with the past and determine if there is the possibility for a future.

Kinsale, Laura.
Lessons in French. 2010. Sourcebooks Casablanca. ISBN 9781402237010. 480pp.

After being jilted three times by the age of 27, Lady Callista Taillefaire has made a life for herself raising bulls and spends much of her time with her prize-winning bull, Hubert. Nine years ago, her father caught Callie in a compromising position with Trevelyn D'Augustin, Duc de Monceaux, and had him sent away. They meet again when Trev returns to Shelford to see his dying mother. The course of true love does not run smoothly; Callie considers a proposal from one of her former suitors, Hubert is lost in a card game, Trev is keeping secrets and neither believes that they have enough to offer the other. Kinsale has penned a multi-layered, funny Regency with quirky secondary characters; readers will adore this couple.

Pettrey, Dani.
Submerged. 2012. Bethany House. ISBN 9780764209826. 320pp.

Bailey Craig has created a new life for herself in Oregon. No one there knows about her past or her reputation. When the aunt who took her in as a teen dies, Bailey has no choice but to return to Yancey, Alaska. She plans to stay just long enough to deal with the Trading Post, the store her aunt has left to her. However, once she gets there, she realizes that her aunt's death was no accident. Bailey's investigation brings her into close contact with Cole McKenna and his siblings. Bailey treated Cole horribly back in high school, and though she hasn't been able to forget about him, she finds it hard to believe that he can see past who she was then. Pettrey's first novel has just the right blend of romance, mystery, and faith. There are a lot of characters (many will get their own stories in later books) but they are well-developed that makes it easy to keep track of them all. (Alaskan Courage, #1)

Teens in Love

Romance isn't just for adults. This list is a sampling of romances featuring teens in a wide variety of settings and situations.

Dessen, Sarah.
  Just Listen. 2006. Viking. ISBN 9780670061051. 384pp.

    Popular teenager Annabel Greene is not excited about the new school year. The summer had been hard for her. Her sister is struggling with an eating disorder, and her mom is battling depression. To top it off, her best friend Sophie won't talk to her and now Annabel finds herself a social outcast. The only one who will listen to Annabel is Owen, another loner and outcast at school. Through her friendship and, subsequent romance, with Owen, Annabel gains the courage to face her problems and to speak out about what happened the night Sophie stopped talking to her.

Echols, Jennifer.
  Dirty Little Secret. 2013. MTV/Galley Books. ISBN 9781451658033. 288pp.

    Bailey has spent the better part of a year rebelling against everything she used to be. Her sister and parents are off touring and promoting Julie's record deal, while Bailey gets to stay home with her grandfather and not play her beloved fiddle. What her parents don't know won't hurt them. With her grandfather's help, she gets a gig playing in a tribute band that plays around Nashville. That leads to another gig and that leads to another. The gigs also lead to Sam. Handsome, exciting, sexy, guitar-playing Sam. Sam isn't content to be play in a tribute band forever. Will he take Bailey along for the ride or dump her like her family did?

Elkeles, Simone.
  Chain Reaction. 2011. Walker. ISBN 9780802727985. 310pp.

    Luis is a fighter, dedicated to his goals and protecting his family. Nikki is the one distraction that could cost him everything. Like his brothers before him, he makes a rash decision in light of learning a family secret that could destroy his newfound happiness with Nikki. Their love for each other though new, is strong. Strong enough to make it through Luis' tangle with the Latino Bloods, who are only too happy to try and seduce Luis into gang life.

Fichera, Liz.
  Hooked. 2013. Harlequin Teen. ISBN 9780373210725. 368pp.

    Fredrika is one of a handful of Native Americans who attend school off the Reservation. Fred's family, like most on the Rez, have it hard. Her dad works as a groundskeeper at the nearby country club and her mom . . . well, she drinks and is mean. Fred's one salvation is golf. With her hand-me-down clubs and patched, horrid, plaid golf bag, she plays as much as she can. Enough that she caught the attention of the coach who signs her onto the team in a heartbeat. The only problem is that it is the boys' team. As if trying to win over a team of resentful boys isn't enough, Fred finds out that hunky Ryan is out to get her for unknowingly getting his best friend kicked off the team to make room for her. While playing and practicing, he gets to know Fred and realizes that he would rather be with her than just about anyone else. He's total country club and she's totally not. Despite that difference, and his ex-girlfriend who wishes she was his current girlfriend, they manage to find a balance that is sweet and sexy.

Fitzpatrick, Huntley.
My Life Next Door. 2012. Dial Books. ISBN 9780803736993. 304pp.

Some people read before bed or watch TV, maybe drink a cup of tea. Not Samantha. She watches the family next door. Their loud, crazy, huge family is a complete turnaround from her solid and, somewhat boring, home life. Her mom is a senator and a bit controlling. Samantha's bedtime viewing is about to become a reality when Jase, the boy next door, hops the fence and starts talking to her. Over the course of the novel, they develop first a deep friendship and then a romantic relationship. Samantha relishes being introduced to, and taken in, as one of the family. Being around Jase's family makes her happy. Being with Jase makes her deliriously happy until an obstacle they may not be able to overcome is put in front of them. Comic relief is provided in the form of four-year-old George, Jase's younger brother.

Howland, Leila.
Nantucket Blue. 2013. Disney Hyperion. ISBN 9781423160519. 294pp.

What could be better than spending the summer with your BFF in beautiful Nantucket? Cricket can't imagine anything better as she and Jules, BFFs since forever, happily plan their summer. That is until tragedy hits Jules's family, and the offer is taken off the table. Determined to have the summer of her life, Cricket heads to Nantucket anyway and takes a job at a cute inn as a chambermaid. Even with Jules ignoring her or maybe because of it, she finds herself drawn to Jules's younger brother Zach, who is totally off limits. Off limits or not, Zach and Cricket finds themselves falling in love as their friendship deepens during the long summer days and even longer summer nights they spend holed up in the inn.

Perkins, Stephanie.
▶ *Anna and the French Kiss*. 2010. Dutton. ISBN 9780525423270. 372pp.

Senior year is supposed to be the best year of high school. Anna is convinced that hers will be great. She has a job she loves and a boy who seems to like her. Things seem perfect. Then her famous author-turned-cheesy movie maker father announces that he is sending Anna to boarding school in Paris for her senior year. Boarding school? Paris? Luckily for Anna, she finds Meredith, Parker, Josh, and St. Clair. Oh, St. Clair . . . he's gorgeous, charming, British/American, and has a girlfriend. The book is filled with moments that have you cheering for Anna and St. Clair as they navigate their way from friends to boyfriend/girlfriend in this realistic, debut novel set in the most romantic city on earth.

Scheidt, Erica Lorraine.
Uses for Boys. 2012. St. Martins Griffin. ISBN 9781250007117. 229pp.

This is a hauntingly beautiful story of Anna and her search for love. Neglected and just about abandoned by her mother in favor of a never-ending stream of boyfriends, husbands and ex-husbands, Anna takes solace in having sex with random boys while trying to be a friend to Toy, the only girl who will still speak to her. Then she meets Sam, who shows her not only what love can be like but also what being a family really means.

Strohm, Stephanie Kate.
Pilgrims Don't Wear Pink. 2012. Houghton Mifflin. ISBN 9780547564593. 204pp.

Self-professed history nerd Libby can't wait for her summer job at Camden Harbor, Maine's oldest living history museum, to start. She is in charge of the Girls of Yesterday Summer Camp. Or, as her annoying roommate calls it, "babysitting." Immediately upon arriving at Camden Harbor, she falls for the most handsome guy around. But life is not all a bed of roses. After deciding that she cannot live with a roommate whom she loathes, Libby moves onto one of the ships docked at the harbor. She begins to wonder if her handsome boyfriend is really the one for her or if her new shipmate and local reporter is more the guy for her. Despite it all, Libby has a great summer and discovers that even nerds can fall in love.

Amnesia

Sometimes it takes losing your memory to find love.

Banks, Maya.
The Darkest Hour. 2010. Berkley. ISBN 9780425227947. 290pp.

When he is notified that his wife Rachel was killed in a plane crash, Navy SEAL Ethan Kelly is devastated. They didn't have the perfect marriage, but he always thought they'd have the time to work things out. On the first anniversary of her death, Ethan receives a package in the mail with information about a kidnapping victim who looks exactly like Rachel and persuades his brothers to go with him to South America to investigate. Rachel has been held prisoner for a year; the drugs that they have forced her to take have caused her to lose most of her memories. The first book in the KGI series is action packed and emotionally satisfying. Banks is known for her steamy hot romances, and this is no exception.

Dreyer, Eileen.
Barely a Lady. 2010. Grand Central Publishing. ISBN 9780446542081. 392pp.

Five years ago, Olivia Grace was ruined when her husband, Jack Wyndham, Earl of Gracechurch, threw her out of their home and divorced her, believing that she had been having an affair. Her latest employer has brought Olivia to Brussels, hoping to find soldiers to marry her daughters. While attending to the wounded on the battlefield at Waterloo, Olivia finds her ex-husband injured and wearing an enemy uniform. When Jack wakes up, he has no memory of the last five years, Olivia pretends to still be happily married to him while trying to determine if Jack has become a traitor. A richly detailed, suspenseful love story, with interesting secondary characters, Dreyer has done her research and it shows. (Drake's Rakes, #1)

Gracie, Anne.
The Accidental Wedding. 2010. Berkley. ISBN 9780425233825. 336pp.

    After her mother's death, Maddy Woodford goes to live in Paris with her grandmother, who taught her to be a lady. When she was 19, her father brought her home from England to care for him on his deathbed and to care for her five half siblings. When Nash Renfrew falls off his horse and knocks himself unconscious, Maddy brings him into her small one bedroom cottage to care for him. When Nash wakes up, they discover that he has amnesia. His memory slowly returns, but Nash can't bear to leave Maddy. He also hopes to catch the person who has been vandalizing Maddy's cottage at night. But Nash's request to stay one more night compromises her. Gracie takes a clichéd storyline and turns it into a charming historical romance. (Devil Riders, #4)

Kellogg, Laurie.
▶ *The Memory of You*. 2012. CreateSpace. ISBN 9781470009663. 238pp.

    After Lieutenant Matt Foster's helicopter goes down in Vietnam, he endures six years of physical and emotional torture in a POW camp. About to be released as part of Operation Homecoming, he is told by the Army that his wife was informed that he was killed in action when his dog tags were found. Matt's memory is gone, he is emotionally damaged, and the broken bones in his face make him unrecognizable. He returns to Redemption, Pennsylvania, planning to leave once he sees for himself that Abby is happy and has moved on with her life. Then Matt learns that they had a son together and he can't just leave, even though Abby is engaged to be married. When they meet, Abby doesn't recognize him but is drawn to him, and when he asks her for a job as a handyman, she agrees. Kellogg pens a heartbreaking love story with a compelling, broken hero and the woman who couldn't forget him. Prequel to the Return to Redemption series.

Naughton, Elisabeth.
Wait for Me. 2012. CreateSpace. ISBN 9781470077891. 280pp.

    Kate's car accident 18 months ago robbed her of her memory. Nothing has felt right to her since, but it isn't until her doctor-husband Jake is killed in a plane crash that she begins to discover why. She finds a photo of a young girl who looks so much like her, but she and Jake didn't have a daughter. As Kate tries to find out more about who she really is, a lead takes her to San Francisco, where she meets Ryan, who lost his wife, Annie, several years ago in a plane crash. Amnesia stories can sometimes be farfetched, but Naughton makes this very believable. While it is clear early on that Kate is Annie, Kate's memory doesn't come back to her right away, and she and Ryan both have to adjust to who she is now. Suspenseful and emotional, with great plotting and some hot sex, don't wait to read this one.

Neville, Miranda.
The Amorous Education of Miss Celia Seaton. 2011. Avon. ISBN 9780062023049. 373pp.

The third book in the Burgundy Club series about a club of rare book collectors features the fashionable Tarquin Compton and the unlucky Celia Seaton. Celia has lost all of her family, a suitor, and her position as governess. She's pretty sure that things can't get worse when she's kidnapped and forced to strip down to a too short shift before being locked in a cottage. While trying to escape the cottage, she stumbles over Tarquin, who ruined her marriage prospects by comparing her to a cauliflower. When she realizes that he has amnesia, Celia sees her chance to get even with him and tells him that he is her fiancé Terence Fish. Tarquin has also lost most of his clothes but has managed to hold onto an erotic book (which really exists in the rare book collection of the British Library) that plays a big part in Celia's education. Neville packs a lot into this witty entertaining love story and puts a fresh spin on many romantic clichés.

Putney, Mary Jo.
Loving a Lost Lord. 2009. Kensington. ISBN 9781420103281. 340pp.

Mariah Clarke's father won Hartley Manor in a card game from George Burke only a few months ago. Burke arrives with news that her father has been murdered and that he intends to get his property back. When he suggests that they should marry, Mariah impulsively tells him that she is already married. Finding Adam Lawford, Duke of Ashton, washed up on the beach with no memory near Hartley Manor is the answer to her prayers. As Adam struggles to regain his memory, he and Mariah fall in love. Adam's friends from the Westerfield Academy (the other Lost Lords) find him, and a secondary plot involves discovering why Adam's steamboat exploded and who is trying to kill him. Putney's *Loving* is a sweet introduction to the Lost Lords series.

Thomas, Sherry.
Tempting the Bride. 2012. Berkley Books. ISBN 9780425251027. 279pp.

Don't say we didn't warn you—Sherry Thomas is difficult to read, only because her writing is so wonderful that afterward you know it is going to be a struggle to find something else worth reading. The Fitzhugh trilogy is no exception. In the final book of the trilogy, Helena Fitzhugh has been having an affair with a married man, and both his family and hers find out. She is sent to America but on her return receives a note asking her to meet him. David Hillsborough, Viscount Hastings, has been in love with Helena since he was 15 but shows his love in much the same way as he did when he was 15—by mocking and teasing her. Helena despises him, but when David finds out that Helena plans to meet her lover at a hotel, he saves her reputation by saying that they have just eloped. Before they can actually marry, Helena has an accident and develops amnesia. Without her memories, Helena likes him and has a chance to get to know the real David, but her memory is starting to return. (Fitzhugh Trilogy, #3)

Love One, Purl Two

Knitting and romance can lead to any number of entanglements.

Betts, Heidi.
Knock Me for a Loop. 2010. St. Martin's Press. ISBN 9780312946739. 340pp.

After Grace finds a puck-bunny in Zack's hotel room, she ends their engagement quite dramatically—a rant about men on her TV show *Amazing Grace,* a baseball bat to his red Hummer, stealing his dog Bruiser and renaming him Muffin. Zack insists he's innocent, but Grace knows what she saw. Months later, Zack is injured and severely depressed, afraid he'll never play hockey again and still missing Grace. Their friends convince Grace to visit him, and she decides to move in and help with his recovery. A light and lively romance. Third in the Chicks with Sticks series. Includes instructions for knitting a dog's sweater.

Bretton, Barbara.
▶ *Casting Spells*. 2008. Berkely Trade. ISBN 9780425223642. 308pp.

Having once been a haven for witches fleeing the Salem Witch Trials, Sugar Maple, Vermont, is now just another sleepy New England town. One that is protected by a charm that is slowly fading and populated solely by supernatural beings. As the spell begins to fade, it leads to the first murder in the town's history. Detective Luke Mackenzie comes to town to investigate, setting up his temporary office next door to the local knitting store. Chloe Hobbs, the half human who owns the local knitting store, needs to find love to come into her powers and to save the town. Trying to be neighborly, the two end up spending quite a bit of time together. Enough time that even though he is 100 percent human, something in Luke's growing love brings out the dormant powers in Chloe. The sparks that fly might just enough to keep the spell going to protect the town. First in the Sugar Maple series, the remainder of the series is more mystery/paranormal than romance. It does, however, follow the continuing story of Luke and Chloe.

Herron, Rachel.
How to Knit a Love Song. 2010. William Morrow. ISBN 9780061841293. 336pp.

Knitting Guru Plays Matchmaker from the Grave. That's what should have been written in Eliza's will but instead it was written that her dear friend, Abigail, should inherit her cottage. The same cottage that is on the land her nephew Cade lives on. Abigail moves to the cottage and in honor of Eliza opens a yarn store. These two never stood a chance. Circumstances throw them together at every opportunity and force them to finally face their feelings for one another.

Ramsay, Hope.
Knit & Stitch. 2013. Forever. ISBN 9781455522279. 384pp.

Mechanic and knitter Molly Canaday is not thrilled when her mother decides to disappear, forcing her to abandon her dreams of opening a body shop to run the family business, a yarn store. Simon Wolfe returns home to Last Chance planning on staying only long enough to settle his late father's affairs. There is magic in the air in Last Chance; it tugs at your heart. Even if your heart has been closed off and, as in both Molly and Simon's case, you are dead set against marriage and long-term relationships. Book 6 in the <u>Last Chance</u> series, this provides updates on previous characters.

Reid, Penny.
Neanderthal Seeks Human. 2013. cipher-naught. ISBN 9780989281003. 402pp.

It would be safe to say that Janie doesn't have the best of luck—not many people lose their apartment and job on the same day that they catch their boyfriend cheating on them. And being escorted from the building by the sexy security guard (Quinn Sullivan aka Sir Handsome McHotpants) that you've had your eyes on is nothing short of humiliating. Janie is quirky and socially inept, prone to bringing up trivial information when she is nervous. Janie keeps running into Quinn and gets a lead on a new job because of him. A cute, sweet romance (with shoes!) that will have you laughing until the tears run down your face. (<u>Knitting in the City</u>, #1)

Ridgway, Christie.
Unravel Me. 2009. Berkley Publishing Group. ISBN 97804252248454. 294pp.

Juliet Weston knew from the time that she was 13 that she would marry the much older General Wayne Weston. What she didn't know was that after just eight years of marriage she would be burying him. Toward the end of his life, Noah Smith helped take care of the general, and when he died, the general asked Noah to take care of Juliet. As Juliet's grief lessens, she finds herself more and more attracted to Noah, but he doesn't think he's good enough for her, and Juliet is still feeling guilty about the general's death. A subplot about Juliet's discovery that her mother conceived her using a sperm donor connects this book with the first and third (about her two sisters) in the <u>Malibu & Ewe</u> series. Ridgway injects humor into serious life and family issues and writes some seriously hot sex scenes.

Wilde, Lori.
The Sweethearts' Knitting Club. 2009. Avon. ISBN 9780061808890. 400pp.

    Mixing love with blackmail is never a good idea. Flynn MacGregor's longtime boyfriend Beau who happens to be sheriff asks her to marry him for the fifth (and last) time. If she says yes, he will cosign for a loan so she can open a yarn shop. If she says yes quickly enough, she might not notice that her old high school boyfriend Jesse is about to be released from jail and is headed straight home to reclaim her heart. The only problem with Beau is that there isn't any passion. With Jesse there is a whole lot of passion. When forced to choose, will she pick the straight and narrow path of a sheriff's wife or take a walk on the wild side with outlaw Jesse?

Baby, oh Baby

Romance and babies don't always go hand in hand, but these couples manage to work around the little ones to find love.

Brown, Carolyn.
The Cowboy's Christmas Baby. 2013. Sourcebooks. ISBN 9781402280498. 352pp.

    Coming home from his tour of duty in Kuwait, Lucas is happy to be home and eager to meet his Internet pen pal, Natalie. Thrilled that she arrives earlier than planned, he is completely unprepared for what he sees when he does spot her. She is brandishing a pistol and carrying a baby on her hip. A baby? Since he has been talking to her for 11 months, he is sure it can't be hers. But Jonah is hers—hers and his best friend Drew's who was killed in battle. Drew is what brought Natalie and Lucas together in the first place. Now it looks as though his son is going to bring them back together. Despite the issue of the baby that Natalie never mentioned, this romance set on a beautiful ranch at Christmas time is sure to capture your heart.

Carr, Robyn.
▶ *Virgin River*. 2007. Mira. ISBN 9780778324904. 386pp.

    Moving from Los Angeles to the tiny town of Virgin River, California, might have been a rash decision for Melinda. Recently widowed and just plain tired of the guilt, the questions, and the sympathetic looks, she needed a change. Virgin River sounded like an ideal getaway, remote, small town in need of a midwife. Sadly the cabin that she was promised as part of her compensation is literally falling down around her. As she plans her quick retreat back to the city, she finds an abandoned baby on her doorstep. How can she leave before she is certain that the baby finds a good home? Of course, she can't. Between the baby on her doorstep and the cute former marine who showed up to help her fix the cabin, she isn't going anywhere anytime soon. A charming romance that showcases the best of small town romances. Continues with *Shelter Mountain*.

Goodman, Jo.
  A Place Called Home. 2011. Zebra. ISBN 9780821774182. 432pp.
    Thea Windham and Mitchell Baker were the maid of honor and best man when Gabe and Kathy got married, and they've seen each other over the years but really don't know each other well. When their friends are killed in an accident, Thea and Mitch find out they've been named joint guardians. Neither is prepared to raise three kids and both have significant others who aren't too excited about taking on someone else's children. Thea is willing to support the kids but has personal reasons for not wanting to have them live with her. Thea and Mitch are attracted to each other, but they have a number of issues to resolve before they can reach their happily ever after. Realistic and romantic, with main characters who are flawed and vulnerable, Goodman has crafted a thoughtful contemporary romance.

Greene, Jennifer.
  Blame It on Cupid. 2007. Harlequin. ISBN 9780373771776. 384pp.
    You can't be held to a promise of guardianship that you wrote on the back of a cocktail napkin, can you? Merry Olsen is about to find out that the answer is yes. When her friend Charlie dies suddenly, she is appointed guardian of his 11-year-old daughter Charlene. Merry has no idea how to be a surrogate mom, especially to an 11-year-old tomboy who is more mature than she is. Luckily her next-door neighbor happens to be a single dad to a set of rambunctious twins. More than that, he is handsome and willing to lend a hand with Charlene. What starts out as lending a helping hand ends up with more than hand holding.

Ladd, Sarah.
  The Heiress of Winterwood. 2013. Thomas Nelson. ISBN 9781401688356. 320pp.
    Life is not easy for Amelia Barrett. She is heiress to her uncle's estate only if she marries by her next birthday, which is in less than two months. She is also struggling to raise Lucy, the daughter of her friend who died shortly after childbirth. Sadly Graham, the child's sea captain father, has taken nearly a year to show up and claim her. Meanwhile Amelia is engaged to a rather unlikeable fellow who makes it clear that he has no interest in raising someone else's brat. When Graham does come home to see that Lucy is cared for properly, Amelia surprises everyone by proposing a marriage of convenience to him. Against his best judgment, Graham accepts knowing that his child will be well taken care of. Society does not take well to this marriage that goes against all the rules. Together they will have to work to prove that they belong together.

London, Julia.
  A Light at Winter's End. 2011. Simon and Schuster. ISBN 9781451606843. 392pp.
    Holly Fisher has never been able to measure up to her older sister, Hannah. She works in a coffee shop, but her passion is song writing. When Hannah

drops off her baby son Mason and disappears, Holly takes him back to the house her mother left her in Cedar Creek, Texas. Holly knows nothing about raising a baby but gets help from her new neighbor, Wyatt Clark, who is raising his daughter Grace. Over playdates, Holly and Wyatt begin to fall in love. London deftly handles a lot of complicated issues—addiction, sibling rivalry, child abandonment, and forgiveness—in this sweet romance. (Cedar Springs, #3)

Ragan, Theresa.
Having My Baby. 2012. CreateSpace. ISBN 9781477501931. 326pp.
   More than anything else, Jill Garrison wants to have a baby. When her fiancé, who can't have children, leaves her at the altar, Jill contacts a sperm bank. Before becoming a football player with the NFL, Derrick Baylor sold sperm when he was desperate for cash. Despite contacting the agency and asking that his sample be destroyed, he receives a letter saying that his profile has been chosen by a client. Derrick tracks Jill down and wants to be part of the baby's life. He starts to fall for Jill but is confused by his feelings because he's been in love with his brother's fiancé Maggie for a long time. This is a sweet story about family, with lots of quirky characters and a wonderful secondary love story.

Thomas, Jodi.
Tall, Dark and Texan. 2008. Jove. ISBN 9780515145134. 293pp.
   At the end of her rope, recently widowed Jessie Barton takes her three daughters and escapes to the one person she believes can save her—Teagen McMurray. A man she knows only through her late husband's letters but she is convinced that he will take her in. And he does. He can't turn her or her girls away. To protect her, he does what any sensible man in his shoes would do—he marries her. To protect her and her girls. At least that is what he tells himself continually while trying to push his growing feelings of love away. When Jessie's past catches up to her, will Teagen prove to be the man she has grown to love as well?

Interesting Occupations

In work, as in love, you have to follow your heart, even when it takes you down an unexpected path.

Admirand, C.H.
Tyler. 2011. Sourcebooks. ISBN 9781402243752. 338pp.
   Tyler always said he would do anything to save the family ranch. Responding to an ad from a local ladies' club, he never dreamed the help they needed would be a male stripper. Then Tyler meets the club's redheaded bookkeeper, Emily, and he can't say no. He can't say much of anything. Having a thing for redheads, his tongue is tied in knots around her. When the club's business is

threatened, Tyler is there to help protect it and Emily. Now if only he could find a way to break through Emily's defenses and show her that he is there for her. (Secret Life of Cowboys, #1)

Brockway, Connie.
No Place for a Dame. 2013. Montlake Romance. ISBN 9781477808580. 292pp.

Beautiful, flame-haired, genius Avery Quinn is the daughter of the former gatekeeper at Killylea. After her father saves the marquess's life, he pays to have Avery educated far beyond what is considered appropriate for a woman. Avery has discovered a comet and wants to become part of the Royal Astronomical Society, but the society is only open to men. After she saves Giles Dalton, the current Marquess of Strand, from a disastrous marriage, she asks for his help in posing as a man. He agrees to sponsor her, as it will provide him with an excuse to be in London, where he plans to search for a missing friend. Once there, he finds that he can't seem to stay away from Avery. Brockway first introduced Giles in *Promise me Heaven* (1994) and he also played a role in *All Through the Night* (1997). It has taken a long time for Brockway to give Giles his own happily ever after, but it is worth the wait.

Carter, Mary.
Accidentally Engaged. 2006. Kensington. ISBN 9780758215390. 304pp.

Psychic Clair Ives hasn't been able to see her own future and, at the age of 32, has been married and divorced three times and has sworn off men. When Rachel, a bride-to-be with cold feet, visits her, she asks Clair to give her a reading telling her not to go through with the wedding. Rachel then leaves behind her engagement ring with a note asking Clair to return it to her fiancé Jake. This is where the fun begins. Arriving at Heron Estates, with Rachel's ring stuck on her finger, Clair is mistaken for Rachel. With the engagement party/business dinner scheduled for that night, Clair is coerced into impersonating Rachel. Jake is handsome, but the best man, Mike, is seriously hot. How long can Clair keep up the charade? Clair is a very unlikely romance heroine, but Carter makes it work. Witty dialogues, quirky characters, and misunderstandings abound in an amusing story that blends mystery and romance.

Duran, Meredith.
The Duke of Shadows. 2008. Pocket Books. ISBN 9781416567035. 371pp.

Betrothed as a child, heiress and artist Emmaline Martin is traveling with her parents to India, when their ship goes down in a storm. Emma, the sole survivor, is rescued by a passing Irish freighter, and when she is brought to her fiancé Marcus Lindley, his primary concerns are whether or not her virtue survived the rescue intact and how soon he can get his hands on her inheritance. Emma quickly grows tired of society—the British in India spend much of their time pretending they're still back in England. Emma meets Julian

Sinclair, Duke of Auburn, a man of mixed Indian and English blood and, as outsiders, they are drawn to one another. When the Sepoy Rebellion occurs, Marcus shows little concern for Emma's safety, and it is Julian who helps her to escape. Several years later, they meet again in England at a showing of Emma's paintings. Both have suffered in the time since they last saw one another, each believing the other to be dead and suffering from the horrors they witnessed during the uprising. Duran depicts a time in history that is not often seen in romance novels; the plot is complex, the characters are compelling, and descriptions of India and England are both evocative and magnificent. *The Duke of Shadows* was the winner of the Gather.com First Chapter Writing Competition.

Enoch, Suzanne.
The Handbook to Handling His Lordship. 2013. St. Martin's Paperbacks. ISBN 9780312534547. 325pp.

After witnessing her employer's murder at the hand of her own husband, Governess Rachel Newbury has no choice but to leave the estate where she was working. Putting the past behind her and changing her name to Emily Portsman, she becomes a Tantalus girl. The Tantalus is a private casino with live-in accommodations for its female employees. Although it has been three years since the murder, Emily still fears that someone will come looking for her and has told no one of her background. Former spy Nathaniel Stokes, the Earl of Westfall, has developed a reputation for finding things discreetly. He is hired by the Marquess of Eberling to track down the woman who stole his wife's necklace and murdered her. When he comes looking for her at the Tantalus, Emily brings him back to her room, hoping that she can seduce him into telling her just how much he knows. Nate and Emily both have their secrets, but they also have incredible chemistry. Neither is looking for love, but sometimes that is when you find it. A clever plot and just enough mystery are guaranteed to keep the reader turning pages. (Scandalous Brides, #4.)

Feehan, Christine.
▶ *Water Bound*. 2010. Jove. ISBN 9780515148244. 480pp.

Someone wants Lev Prakenskii dead. He's been thrown overboard and left to drown, when he is rescued by Rikki Sitmore, a sea urchin diver. Rikki has experienced a lot of tragedy in her life, related to a series of fires that she's not sure she didn't set. Rikki has found refuge in the coastal town of Sea Haven, after jointly purchasing a farm with a small group of women she met during grief counseling. Rikki's autism makes everyday life more challenging, and bringing Lev to her home to care for him disrupts her routines, but there is something about him that compels her to be there for him. Lev is equally captivated by her. Rich characterization, an action-packed plot, steamy sex scenes, and magical elements keep this story moving along. This is the first book in the Sisters of the Heart series, but Sea Haven will be instantly recognizable to readers who enjoyed Feehan's Drake Sisters series.

Herkness, Nancy.
Shower of Stars. 2004. Berkley. ISBN 9780425197110. 320pp.

Meteorite hunter Jack Lanette has discovered the find of a lifetime, a rock that may provide proof of life on Mars. Generally avoiding all publicity, Jack knows that an interview will send the price soaring and agrees to an interview with Mr. Charlie Berglund from the *New York Times*. When Charlie arrives at his door asking that he help her with a dog who was hit by a car, Jack is surprised to find that she is a woman. Charlie is desperate to have a baby but has been told by her social worker that her freelance career traveling and writing adventure stories isn't helping her case. When Charlie is finally able to interview Jack, she realizes that writing a book about him might be the answer to her problems. Jack doesn't want anyone looking too deeply into his past and offers to marry Charlie instead. Will their love shine brightly, or will it be eclipsed by their secrets?

Roberts, Nora.
The Search. 2010. Putnam Adult. ISBN 9780399156571. 488pp.

Ten years ago, Fiona Barstow was the only survivor of the Red Scarf Killer, but before the police could catch him, he killed her fiancé Greg and his K-9 partner. She moved to Orcas Island, off the coast of Washington, to rebuild her life. Fiona has become a dog trainer and volunteers with the search and rescue unit on the island. She has three dogs: Peck, Bogart, and Newman. Woodworker Simon Doyle enters her life, desperate for some help with his new puppy Jaws. When a copycat killer surfaces, the police suspect that Fiona will be on his victim list. As Fiona trains Jaws and Simon, a relationship develops between them, despite their being opposites in nearly every way. If you've read Nora Roberts before, you will have some idea of what you're getting; details of dog training and search and rescue operations are woven into the fabric of this romance. The four dogs get plenty of page time, and Jaws, in particular, offers several comedic moments.

We've Got Issues

Stock up on the giant-size box of tissues. These couples have more issues than National Geographic, but somehow they manage to overcome them and find love and happiness.

Drake, Laura.
The Sweet Spot. 2013. Forever. ISBN 9781455521951. 336pp.

Charla Rae Denny and Jimmy (JB) were high school sweethearts and had the perfect marriage until they lost their only child in a tragic accident. Afterward, Charla turned to valium, and when JB's repeated efforts to get through to her failed, he turned to a blonde half his age. Things get worse for Charla, as her father's Alzheimer's progresses and she almost loses the ranch. JB wants to repair their damaged relationship, but has too much happened for them to ever be happy together again? A heart-wrenching story about the power of forgiveness, endearing secondary characters, and more fascinating details about bulls than I ever thought I'd want to know. It's not a light read, but the humor and growth of the characters are worth the time invested.

Force, Marie.
Hoping for Love. 2012. eBook by HTJB, Inc. ISBN 9780615824352. 294pp.

After having lap-band surgery and losing more than 100 pounds, pharmacist Grace Ryan is no longer the "fat girl," but she hasn't outgrown her decades-long crush on Trey. When she refuses to sleep with him, Trey leaves her stranded on Gansett Island after the last ferry and without her purse or a dollar to her name. Singer/songwriter Evan McCarthy notices Grace crying and comes to her rescue. They are drawn to each other, but Evan doesn't do relationships and plans to return to Nashville soon. Grace may have transformed on the outside, but she's still dealing with a lot of self-esteem issues. Evan is also dealing with his own issues, including fear of commitment and stage fright. Force writes very realistic characters who will steal your heart, and the love scenes are both sexy and sweet. In the fifth book of the McCarthys of Gansett Island series, you'll have the chance to catch up on characters from previous books while being introduced to new couples who will be featured in later books.

Longley, Barbara.
Far from Perfect. 2012. Montlake Romance. ISBN 978161285897. 350pp.

Noah Langford is lucky to be alive after a bombing in Iraq takes his leg and ends his military career. When his stepbrother dies in in a car accident, he discovers that Matt left behind an ex-girlfriend and a baby. Ceejay Lovejoy's life is far from perfect, despite living in Perfect, Indiana. Her mother abandoned her as a child, and when she got pregnant, her boyfriend took her life savings and her car. Ceejay, with the help of the aunt who raised her, has worked her way through nursing school and is planning to move to a big city and leave her past behind. Noah is suffering from posttraumatic stress disorder and, not knowing what he wants to do with his life, decides to travel to Indiana and meet Ceejay. As he gets to know her, he thinks they may have a future together, but the secrets he's keeping may ruin their chances. The first book in the Perfect, Indiana, series is emotional and moving; the characters are strong and well developed.

McGarry, Katie.
Pushing the Limits. 2012. Harlequin Teen. ISBN 9780373210497. 416pp.

Echo Emerson doesn't remember the night her mother tried to kill her or how she wound up with the scars on her arms. Noah Hutchins wants to get custody of his two younger brothers when he turns 18. They meet when the counsellor they are both ordered to see sets Echo up as Noah's tutor. Told in alternating chapters, readers get to see both sides of their love story and how they grow and heal, as they finish their senior year of high school.

Shalvis, Jill.
Head over Heels. 2011. Forever. ISBN 9780446571630. 350pp.

Chloe Traeger and her sisters inherited a house from their mother in Lucky Harbor, which they are converting into a bed and breakfast. The sisters don't know each other well—they have different fathers, and Chloe was the only one raised by their mother, Phoebe. Due to her upbringing, Chloe has turned out to be a bit of a wild child with a knack for getting into trouble. Sheriff Sawyer Thompson is probably the last person she should consider getting involved with, but she is drawn to the former bad boy. Chloe has severe asthma, which has caused her love life to suffer, as she has to decide before sex if a guy is inhaler worthy. Sawyer is definitely worth the inhaler, and the sex scenes are hot! Chloe and Sawyer both have to resolve family issues while figuring out if they are ready to settle down. Sisterly bonding, witty dialogues, and a great bromance make the third Lucky Harbor book a winner.

Thomas, Jodi.
Chance of a Lifetime. 2012. Berkley. ISBN 9780425250525. 336pp.

Thomas tells the story of three different couples in the fifth installment in the Harmony series. The main story centers around local librarian, Emily Tomlinson, who survived a brutal attack when she was in high school that ended her friendship with Tanner Parker, who believes it was his fault. When Tanner asks for a favor, their friendship is rekindled and may turn into something more. New lawyer, Rick Matheson, is plagued by a series of accidents that may not be accidental when Trace Adams, U.S. Marshall rides into town on her motorcycle. Rick can't figure out why anyone would target him and wants to solve the mystery so that he has a future to share with Trace. Aspiring musician Beau Yates is well on his way to making it big. Not yet 21, he's got a regular gig at one of the local bars, where he has several dreamlike encounters with a girl he knows only as Trouble who drives a red sports car. Visiting Harmony is like coming home to a place where everybody knows your name. Thomas builds a world that you can imagine exists out there somewhere, peopled with characters you grow to love and wish you knew in real life.

Wiggs, Susan.
▶ *Just Breathe*. 2008. Mira. ISBN 9780778325772. 469pp.

Although she's having a hard time getting pregnant, Chicago cartoonist Sarah Moon feels that she has a pretty good life; her husband Jack is doing well after treatment for testicular cancer and her comic strip *Just Breathe* is in syndication. After going to another fertility treatment by herself, Sarah stops by Jack's work site with a pizza and discovers that he's been cheating on her. Sarah returns to her family's oyster farm in California and begins a relationship with her high school nemesis, firefighter Will Bonner, and his stepdaughter,

Aurora, who reminds Sarah of her younger self. Sarah finally feels like she's getting her life back together when she discovers she's pregnant. Each section of the book starts with one of Sarah's comic strips. Readers will laugh and cry as they follow Sarah's journey to find herself after losing everything she thought was important.

Somebody Else's Wedding

Weddings, whether yours or someone else's, are full of drama, sometimes comedy, and, of course, love and romance.

Barth, Christi.
Friends to Lovers. 2013. Carina Press. ISBN 9781426896507. 228pp. (eBook)
>   When the lights go out on New Year's Eve, Daphne Lowell, florist and wedding planner, takes it as a sign and gives in to the attraction she has long felt and kisses her best friend and notorious womanizer Gibson Moore. It was everything she hoped it would be and more. Except that when the lights come on, she disappears before Gibson could figure out who the mystery woman kissing him was. Gibson has no idea who the mystery woman was, but he is determined to find out as it was the best kiss of his life. Going from friends to lovers is a big leap, but with a bit of help from an aphrodisiac food tasting, they manage to make the leap without too much collateral damage. (Aisle Bound, #3).

Bowman, Valerie.
Secrets of a Runaway Bride. 2013. St. Martin's. ISBN 9781250008961. 384pp.
>   Annie Andrews is sure that Arthur Eggleston will marry her if she could just convince him that she is the right woman for him. How can she possibly do that if Jordan Holloway, Earl of Ashbourne and annoyingly charming best friend and brother-in-law of her sister, won't leave her alone? Annie is sure that her sister put Jordan to the task solely so that she can enjoy her honeymoon worry free. Jordan tries in vain to keep Annie from eloping, but somewhere along the way he loses his heart to her. (Secret Brides, #2)

Bricker, Sandra.
Always the Baker, Finally the Bride. 2013. Abingdon Press. ISBN 978142673 2270. 352pp.
>   After having helped many brides design their wedding cakes, Emma Rae is finally getting to design her own. She and Jackson, the owner of the Tangle-wood Inn where she works, are getting married. Well, they are trying to get married. Things go from bad to worse as a surprising offer to buy Tanglewood and a potential move out of the country are put on the table. In spite of all the craziness and uncertainty at Tanglewood, the one thing that doesn't waver is Emma and Jackson's love for each other or their faith in God. With those two

things firmly in hand, they can handle anything that comes their way. A sweet and fun romance with beautiful wedding cake sketches and delicious recipes! (Emma Rae Creations, #4)

Higgins, Kristan.
Best Man. 2013. HQN Books. ISBN 9780373777921. 432pp.

Faith Holland's fairytale romance ended at the altar when her fiancé admitted in front of all of their family and friends that he is gay. She goes on their honeymoon alone and doesn't return to tiny Manningsport, New York, for three and a half years. Faith has become a successful landscape architect, and she's got big plans for restoring the barn behind her family's winery. She finds herself drawn to the town's police chief, Levi Cooper, but has a hard time forgetting that he was Jeremy's best friend and encouraged him to come out of the closet. Higgins hits all the right notes in this romantic comedy, but there are many elements that will tug at your heart strings. The perspective shifts back and forth between Faith and Levi, allowing the reader to fully experience their story. A secondary plot line involving Faith's older sister and her husband, which details their attempts to "bring sexy back," will leave you laughing until the tears stream down your face. First in a projected trilogy.

Mansell, Jill.
▶ *Walk in the Park*. 2012. Sourcebooks. ISBN 9781402269943. 437pp.

Lara Carson is heading back to Bath for her father's funeral. She hasn't been back in 18 years. She left without a trace. Nobody knew where she went. Not her best friend Evie, nor her then boyfriend Flynn. Now after the funeral, Evie asks her to stay for her wedding. Lara can't say no to her old friend. News travels fast, and soon all of Bath knows that Lara is back and has a secret. Sure enough she runs into Flynn and is forced to reveal her secret to him—her 18-year-old secret named Gigi. As they navigate the path of co-parenting, it is hard to ignore the sparks that still exist between them. They sweetly rediscover their love for one another.

Phillips, Susan Elizabeth.
Call Me Irresistible. 2010. William Morrow. ISBN 9780061351525. 387pp.

Taking beloved characters from previous books, Phillips creates a romance that fans are sure to love. The free-spirited daughter of Hollywood legends, Meg Koranda is in Wynette, Texas, for best friend and daughter of former U.S. president Lucy Jorik's wedding to former golf pro and mayor Ted. Sadly Meg convinces Lucy to call the wedding off at the very last minute and in doing so turns herself into persona non grata in Wynette. The residents of Wynette do not take kindly to their golden boy being turned into a laughingstock. Now Meg is stranded in town with no way out and a town full of people who hate her. Meg is on her own to figure out a way to mend the fences with not just Lucy but Ted, too. As she does, she begins to see Ted as the town does, as the golden boy. Falling for him was not part of her plan, but when it comes to the heart, there are no plans. (Wynette, Texas, #6)

Sherwood, Pamela.
Waltz with a Stranger. 2012. Sourcebooks. ISBN 9781402273223. 434pp.

Preferring to hide in the shadows where her scar and limp aren't as noticeable, American heiress Aurelia Newbold watches while the rest of London is charmed by her twin sister Amelia. One notable exception to that is James Trelawney. Being without a title or wealth, he is doing his best to hide in the shadows also. A shared waltz between them changes everything for Aurelia. She decides to go to a spa in France to work on her recovery. When she comes back to London a year later, she is surprised to learn that her sister is engaged to her once-upon-a-time dance partner. For his part, James is now an earl, having inherited his late cousin's estate and title. He is just as surprised as to see Aurelia again. There is some mystery surrounding the death of James's cousin that adds to the story. No evil twins here; Amelia loves her twin and only wants the best for her. Does she want that enough to step aside and let Aurelia explore a relationship with James?

Thompson, Janice A.
Picture Perfect. 2013. Revell. ISBN 9780800721527. 336pp.

The first book in a series spun off from the author's popular Weddings by Bella series finds wedding photographer Hannah McDermott trying her hardest to win over wedding planner Bella and land the job of photographing THE wedding of the year. Her biggest rival is the very handsome and distracting Drew Kincaid. The McDermott–Kincaid feud raged back in the old country for ages. Hannah and Drew have been in competition for what seems like forever. It looks like Drew and Hannah might be the ones to bring around a cease-fire. Just as the flames are beginning to burn for them, their competition turns first to friendship and then to more. (Weddings by Design, #1)

Wilde, Lori.
Once Smitten, Twice Shy. 2008. Forever. ISBN 9780446618465. 324pp.

When the going gets tough, Tish Gallagher goes shopping. Things can't get tougher. Her wedding photography business is almost a bust, her cable is getting turned off, her credit cards are getting cut up, and her car is getting repoed. In a last ditch attempt to save her business and her credit rating, she makes a wish on an antique wedding veil that is supposed to grant your deepest wish. The veil must have major good-luck mojo because soon after Tish is called to photograph the president's daughter's wedding. Her luck is turning! First Daughter Elysee Benedict is marrying Secret Service Agent Shane Tremont, who just happens to be Tish's smoldering ex-husband, whom she is still completely in love with. Turns out that Shane isn't quite over Tish either. (Wedding Veil Wishes, #2)

Woods, Sherryl.
Sea Glass Island. 2013. Mira. ISBN 9780778314462. 400pp.

Two out of the three Castle sisters have found love. Could it be eldest sister Samantha's turn now? As she and the family gather at Sand Castle Bay for sister Emily's wedding, thoughts naturally turn toward fixing up Samantha, the maid of honor, with the best man. That might not be so bad if the best man in question wasn't Samantha's high school crush Ethan Cole. For Ethan, he isn't eager to be part of the matchmaking. A war hero who lost a leg in Afghanistan, he has given up on love after his fiancée gave up on him when he came home. As they spend time together, Samantha realizes that her teenage crush is turning into full-blown love. Couples from the previous two books make appearances and their storylines are tied up, but this can easily be read as a stand-alone. (Ocean Breeze, #3)

All Quiet on the Home Front

It's not all ticker-tape and parades when soldiers return, and the transition from war to a return home is not always an easy one to make. Family is not always there for you, and romantic relationships sometimes don't survive the war. These heroes suffer greatly, but they all find love.

Clare, Pamela.
Defiant. 2012. Berkley. ISBN 9780425246115. 364pp.

Lady Sarah Woodville has been sent to New York from her home in England after a scandal that ruined her reputation beyond repair. Traveling with a chaperone, she is captured by the Shawnee during the French and Indian War. Major Connor MacKinnon is ordered by his commanding officer Lord William Wentworth to rescue his niece, Lady Sarah. The only way that Connor can secure her freedom from the Shawnee warrior is to claim her for himself. Without question, he does this and then begins to learn who this spirited brave lass is who is now acting as his wife. Sarah is surprised at the affection she feels toward her rescuer. When they finally return to her uncle's home, neither is prepared for the reaction to their budding romance and both vow to fight for it no matter the cost. Connor's relationship with his brothers (featured in previous books) is funny and touching, while the romance between Sarah and Connor is tender and very sensual. An unusual setting for historical romance is brought to life by Clare. (MacKinnon's Rangers trilogy, #3)

Gerard, Cindy.
The Way Home. 2013. Gallery Books. ISBN 9781476735207. 336pp.

Four years ago, nurse Jess Albright's husband is killed in Afghanistan. She decides to return home to the small Minnesota town where she grew up and work in the family store. Over a year ago, a kidnapping brought Tyler Brown, a former special ops soldier, to town, and there seemed to be a spark between them, but she never heard from him. He returns to Minnesota and they are just starting to fall in love when Jess learns that her husband, J.R. is still alive but has amnesia. He was rescued by Rabia, a widowed Afghan woman, after an explosion. She had been hiding him from the Taliban when his memories slowly began to return, but he still has no memory of his life before the explosion. We don't want to give anything away in this review, but there is a happily ever after or two. Gerard's writes realistic characters, and this is a heartbreaking story with elements of romantic suspense.

Harrington, Alexis.
Home by Nightfall. 2012. Montlake Romance. ISBN 9781612182063. 287pp.
  Susannah Braddock is one of many wives whose husbands didn't return from the front in World War I. Her husband Riley was killed in France. Trying to move on with her life, she turns to the day-to-day operations of the family horse farm and to Tanner Grenfell. Tanner is a trusted friend and has helped run the farm during Riley's absence. All seems to be moving in the right direction as the two marry and settle down to raise Tanner's nephews, until Riley returns home with no memory of his wife or anything that happened before the war. With a new family and husband and a husband who has returned from the dead, what is a girl to do? Susannah faces a heart wrenching decision in this dramatic romance.

Morgan, Victoria.
For the Love of a Soldier. 2013. Berkley. ISBN 9780425264232. 336pp.
  Disguising herself as a man, Lady Alexandra Langdon takes to the gaming tables and risks her last few pounds in a desperate attempt to replenish her funds. She loses to Captain Garrett Sinclair, Earl of Kendall, a survivor of the Charge of the Light Brigade. Something about the young man makes Garrett decide to refuse his money. Alex later warns Garrett that someone is plotting to murder him and that they work together to uncover his would-be killer. Garrett soon realizes that Alex is not a man but a beautiful young woman in a desperate situation. Morgan's debut novel is beautifully written, the hero and heroine have amazing chemistry, and the description of the Battle of Balaclava makes for fascinating reading.

Pappano, Marilyn.
A Hero to Come Home to. 2013. Forever. ISBN 9781455520046. 384pp.
  Army veteran Staff Sergeant Dane Clark lost a leg in Afghanistan; since then he has tried to forget his ex-wife and move on with his new life. At the same time, third-grade teacher Carly Lowry is trying to move past the death of her husband Jeff in Afghanistan almost two years ago. Through her friends in the Fort Murphy Widows Club, she learns to live again and ultimately to love again. Dane hasn't told Carly everything; will she leave him too when she learns the secret he's been keeping? Pappano handles Carly's struggle to love again masterfully; neither Jeff nor Dane are perfect people, but they are

both perfect for Carly at a particular time in her life. First in the <u>Tallgrass</u> series.

Ross, JoAnn.
The Homecoming. 2010. Penguin. ISBN 9780451230676. 377pp.

    Former bad boy-turned-Navy SEAL Sax Doucett returns home to Shelter Bay, Oregon, to rebuild his life after the rest of his unit is killed during a mission in Afghanistan. He is haunted by dreams about his SEAL teammates. When his dog finds a human bone on the beach during an evening walk, Sax reconnects with his high school crush, Sheriff Kara Conway. Kara fell in love with her husband Jared back when they were still in grade school. Shortly after Jared is killed answering a domestic violence call, Kara's father dies in a suspicious hunting accident. Kara returns to Shelter Bay to take over her father's position as sheriff and provide her young son with a safe, quiet place to grow up. The romance between Kara and Sax develops slowly, while long buried secrets come to light. A secondary romance and strong family relationships also play a big part in the first book in the <u>Shelter Bay</u> series.

Snow, Heather.
Sweet Madness. 2013. Penguin. ISBN 9780451239679. 384pp.

    The third and final book in the <u>Veiled Seduction</u> series opens with a ball to celebrate Lady Penelope marriage to the hero's cousin. Two and a half years later, after her husband's suicide, Penelope is visiting Gabriel Devereux, Marquis of Bromwich, at Vickering Place, the asylum his family sent him to after a series of violent episodes. His experiences in the Napoleonic Wars have left their mark on him. Penelope has a knack for helping men with "battle fatigue," the historical term for posttraumatic stress disorder (PTSD). Gabriel is skeptical of Penelope's ability to help him, but eventually she convinces him to let her try. Their work together heals her, too, as she has suffered from guilt for being unable to prevent Michael's suicide. Snow writes complex, multidimensional characters, and this compelling passionate love story combines a tortured hero and an intelligent, strong woman in a unique way, giving the reader insight into historical theories about and treatments for mental illness and PTSD.

Stewart, Mariah.
▶ *Hometown Girl*. 2011. Ballantine. ISBN 9780345531216. 374pp.

    It's been two years since Brooke Madison Bowers's husband was killed while serving in Iraq. She returned to her hometown of St. Dennis, Maryland, and the support of all of her family and friends, and has been trying to rebuild her life—going to school, taking care of her son, starting a cupcake business, but after marrying and losing the man of her dreams, she's not sure that she wants another relationship. Jesse Enright moves to St. Dennis to earn a position in his grandfather's law firm. Jesse's father was disbarred for embezzlement and Jesse has to prove himself. When Jesse meets Brooke, he knows that she is the one for him, but can he convince her that it is possible to have two loves in a lifetime? Colorful characters, strong community ties, and a quaint seaside town make the fourth book in the <u>Chesapeake Diaries</u> series a winner.

Second Chance at Love

If at first you don't succeed, try, try again. Not everyone is first-time lucky when it comes to love, but all of these couples get their chance at love.

Ashford, Jane.
Once Again a Bride. 2013. Sourcebooks Casablanca. ISBN 9781402276729. 384pp.

Unhappily married to a man more than 30 years her senior, Charlotte Wylde finally has her freedom when her husband is murdered by thieves. Before his death, he spent most of her fortune on his collection of antiquities and made a provision in his will that she could only stay if the house is turned into a museum and she acts as a tour guide. Sir Alexander Wylde, Henry's much younger nephew, is shocked by his murder and even more shocked to discover Henry's beautiful young widow. It takes time for Charlotte and Alec to learn to trust each other, especially when Charlotte is accused of being involved in the murder. With a nod toward *Upstairs, Downstairs* and *Downton Abbey,* the secondary romance involving Charlotte's maid Lucy and Alec's footman Ethan gets almost as much page time in this delightful Regency.

Brogan, Tracy.
Crazy Little Thing. 2012. Montlake Romance. ISBN 9781612186009. 342pp.

After her divorce, Sadie Turner decides to spend the summer regrouping at her kooky Aunt Dody's house on the shores of Lake Michigan. A perfectionist, whose life is far from perfect at the moment, Sadie jumps at the chance to become a professional organizer, spending her downtime on the beach with her two young kids. A fling with the doctor next door might be just the thing to boost her confidence, but the relationship between Sadie and Des starts to become something more. Aunt Dody and gay cousin Fontaine are hilarious, and Sadie is constantly getting herself into embarrassing situations. If you need cheering up or just want to laugh, this is a great romance to curl up with.

Higgins, Kristan.
▶ *The Next Best Thing*. 2010. HQN Books. ISBN 97803733774388. 400pp.

After her husband Jimmy is killed in a car accident only a few months after their marriage, Lucy Lang believes in the family curse. Her mother and her aunts (the Black Widows) also lost their husbands at a young age. It's been five years since Jimmy died, and Lucy decides it is time to move on with her life. This means giving up her friends-with-benefits relationship with Ethan, who is also her brother-in-law. Lucy wants a husband and children but doesn't want to fall in love again. Ethan introduced Jimmy to Lucy and has been in love with her since they first met. Is it possible that the man Lucy is looking for has been there all along? Higgins has mastered the humorous, small-town romance and pens wonderful secondary characters that add to the plot; all of her characters are so real that you feel like you've lost a friend when you finish her books.

Jackson, Lisa, Lamb, Cathy, Chamberlin, Holly, and Noonan, Rosalind.
Beach Season. 2011. Kensington. ISBN 9780758265630. 481pp.

These four novellas offer second chances by the sea. Shawna's fiancé, Parker, was in a car accident and doesn't remember her. She is determined that they will have a second chance in Jackson's *The Brass Ring*. June MacKenzie makes beautiful lace wedding dresses, but after leaving her cheating ex, she will never wear one. Then she meets songwriter Reece in June's *Lace by Lamb*. After a bad marriage, Thea meets her first love in a local diner while on vacation in Chamberlain's *Second Chance Sweethearts*. Noonan's Carolina Summer has Jane Doyle in a hurry to get away from New York, but the Outer Banks and a sexy sheriff have her wanting to stay awhile.

March, Emily.
Angel's Rest. 2011. Ballantine Books. ISBN 9780345518347. 336pp.

Moving from suspense to contemporary romance and changing her name, Geralyn Dawson has penned a new Callahan brother book under the name Emily March. The tiny mountain town of Eternity Springs, Colorado, offers those in need a place to heal. Gabe Callahan lost everything—first his identity in a Sarajevo prison and then his wife and young son in a tragic accident. A dog caught in a trap brings him into contact with vet Nicole Sullivan. After her marriage ended in divorce, Nicole came home to Eternity Springs to regroup and start over. The dog keeps bringing Gabe and Nicole together, but is Gabe too wounded to love again? A small town, light mystery and tortured hero add up to the start of a great new series. (Eternity Springs, #1)

McCarthy, Erin.
Flat Out Sexy. 2008. Berkley. ISBN 9780425224076. 291pp.

After her husband Pete is killed during a NASCAR race, Tamara Briggs vowed to stay away from drivers. She wants to find someone safe. At a cocktail party with just that kind of man, she spills her wine on rookie driver, Elec Monroe. The chemistry is intense, and after dumping her date, they spend the night together. But while Tamara's not interested in a relationship with him, especially after discovering he's a mere 25 to her 32, he wants to meet her children. A quick read full of smoldering sex scenes and humor, this is the first in the Fast Track series.

Phillips, Carly.
Serendipity. 2011. Berkley. ISBN 9780425243831. 283pp.

Ethan Barron and Faith Harrington both have something to prove when they return home to Serendipity, New York, after long absences. Faith's father was convicted of running a Ponzi scheme and her marriage crumbled; she's hoping for a fresh start and plans to open an interior design business. Ethan Barron left town right after his parents were killed in an accident on their way to bail him out. He wants to repair his relationship with his younger brothers and purchases the Harrington house to show them that he's capable of settling down. Wanting to establish herself, Faith can't afford to turn down Ethan's request that she redecorate her childhood home for him. The arrival of a teenage half-sister that Ethan didn't know he had creates an opportunity to reestablish relationships with his brothers but gets in the way of a relationship with Tess. Family dramas, hot sex, a sweet romance, well-developed characters—this book has it all. Readers will be happy to know that each of Ethan's brothers has their own book in the Serendipity series.

Selvig, Lizbeth.
The Rancher and the Rock Star. 2012. Avon Impulse. ISBN 9780062134653. 432pp.

Debut author Selvig pens a sweet, engaging romance between a widowed rancher and a rock legend. Abby Stadler has been struggling for a long time, but she's proud of the fact that she's been able to raise her teenage daughter without asking for help from anyone. Her quiet life becomes a whole lot more interesting when Kim's Facebook friend comes to visit and she agrees to hire him to help out with their horse farm. Then Gray Covey shows up at her door—the Gray Covey, her daughter Kim's favorite rock star. Gray is used to life going according to schedule and hunting down his missing 16-year-old son, Dawson, and staying on a horse farm for the next six weeks to rebuild their relationship is not part of his plan. The love story builds slowly—Abby doesn't know how to accept someone's help, and Gray has to learn how to earn someone's love. A heartwarming story about family, friendship, and trust; the secondary characters are quirky and charming; and the small-town setting will make you feel right at home.

Marriage by Mistake

Accidents happen—they don't usually result in a wedding, but when they do, if you make the best of it, you might just find love.

Alexander, Victoria.
Secrets of a Proper Lady. Avon. 2007. ISBN 9780060882648. 384pp.

The Earl of Marsham and American businessman Harold Sinclair make a deal to marry off their children to shore up their businesses and increase their cash flow. Daniel Sinclair and Lady Cordelia have not met, and neither is pleased to find this out. Cordelia masquerades as her companion, Ms. Sara Palmer, and makes an appointment with Mr. Sinclair's secretary, Warren Lewis, to find out about the man she is being forced to marry. The day of the meeting,

Mr. Lewis is sick and Daniel meets "Sara." "Sara" and "Warren" fall for each other, but they each know that due to their family situation they cannot marry. A double case of mistaken identity makes for some really entertaining situations, especially when they each find out the truth, but don't realize that the other knows. (Last Man Standing, #3)

Anderson, Catherine.

▶ *Lucky Penny*. 2012. Signet. ISBN. 9780451236036. 432pp.

Before she died, Brianna O'Keefe promised her twin sister that she would raise her daughter Daphne as her own. She leaves Boston and accepts a job on a Colorado ranch; to avoid unwanted attention, she tells her new employer that her husband is a Denver gold miner. When her employer marries, he forces her to write letters to her husband. When David Paxton, the Marshall of No Name, Colorado, shows up, Briana insists that her husband is another David Paxton. David had already used his connections to search for another man by that name unsuccessfully. He was a bit of a hell-raiser in his younger years, and it is possible that he fathered a child, but no matter how drunk he might have been, he can't believe he forgot getting married. Daphne bears an uncanny resemblance to David's mother, right down to the family birthmark. Brianna tries to convince David that Daphne is not her daughter, but he doesn't believe her. They take the case before a judge, who is somewhat less than sober, and he pronounces them man and wife, giving David the right to take them home to his ranch. The romance between David and Brianna builds slowly against the backdrop of Colorado in 1891. Anderson touches on the social issues of the time and explores the meaning of family. Although it is part of the Paxton family series, *Lucky Penny* can be read as a stand-alone novel.

Hunter, Denise.

The Accidental Bride. 2012. Thomas Nelson. ISBN 9781595548023. 304pp.

Fourteen years ago, Shay Brandenberger was left in her wedding gown on the courthouse steps waiting for her groom, Travis McCoy. Still living in Moose Creek, Montana, Shay is now a single mother raising her 12-year-old daughter and struggling to make the payments on her ranch. She agrees to play the bride in the annual Founder's Day reenactment but gets the shock of her life when she walks down the aisle and Travis is at the end of it. When the marriage certificate they signed years ago is filed by mistake, Shay becomes an accidental bride. Could this be God's way of answering her prayers? Endearing characters, witty dialogues, and descriptive settings make for a truly enjoyable sweet romance. (Big Sky Romances, #2)

Linden, Carolyn.

What a Gentleman Wants. 2006. Zebra. ISBN 9780821779316. 351pp.

Marcus Reese, the Duke of Exeter, has spent much of his life cleaning up his twin brother's mistakes. Most recently, David proposed a marriage of convenience to the widow of a vicar who has a young daughter to take care of, but signed Marcus's name to the marriage license. Hannah and Marcus struggle to find a way out of their sham marriage, but when the wedding announcement is sent to the papers, Marcus's mother and sister arrive in town, thrilled that Marcus has finally settled down. Marcus offers Hannah a cottage and a settlement that will ensure her independence if she will agree to the pretend marriage for the remainder of the season. Compelling secondary characters and a suspenseful subplot make for a delightful Regency romance. (Reece Family, #1)

Parra, Nancy J.
The Counterfeit Bride. 2011. Montlake Romance. ISBN 9781477811740. 188pp.
No one is more surprised than Lillian Picken when her husband, Donovan West, returns from the Army. In 1877, Silverton, Colorado, women weren't able to own their own stores, so Lillian had invented a husband. Patrick Donovan is a member of the newly created secret service and posing as the pretty redhead's husband provides him with a cover story while he investigates a ring of counterfeiters. Fast paced and funny with a strong, capable heroine.

Skye, Christina.
The Accidental Bride. 2012. HQN Books. ISBN 9780373776597 384pp.
All of Jilly O'Hara's dreams are about to come true—she's just opened her own restaurant and created her own line of organic salsas. After fainting in the middle of dinner service, her doctors warn that she has to slow down. Her best friends Caro, Grace, and Olivia send her to a resort in Wyoming for a little R and R. Arriving at the airport outside of Lost Creek, it is love at first sight for Jilly and Winslow; then Jilly notices the chocolate labs' attractive owner, Walker Hale. Lost Creek is the ideal place for Jilly to heal and rethink her life's plans. Walker and Winslow did two tours with the marines before they were both injured. Now Walker spends much of his time in his secluded mountain cabin, but after running into Jilly in town, he seems to be spending a lot more time in Lost Creek. Jilly and Walker allow themselves to be talked into an outrageous plan to marry when a lavish wedding scheduled at the resort is canceled, but what will happen when Jilly decides that she doesn't want to be just an accidental bride? Skye's portrayal of small-town life will leave you wishing for a week at Lost Creek the next time life gets hectic. (Summer Island, #2)

Warren, Tracy Anne. ♛
The Husband Trap. 2006. Ivy Books. ISBN 9780345483089. 358pp.
Adrian Winter, the Duke of Raeburn, believes that he has just married Jeannette Rose Brantford, the most beautiful girl this season, in a fabulous wedding with all of the Ton in attendance. To save the family from disgrace when Jeannette refuses to marry Adrian, her twin sister Violet agrees to marry him instead. Adrian is pleased to see that Jeannette has matured and finds himself falling in love with his wife. Violet has long been in love with Adrian from afar, and, as she gets to know him better, she falls more deeply in love with him. Adrian sometimes feels that Violet is two different women, at times very outgoing and

moments later, shy and quiet. He also senses that she is keeping secrets from him. What will happen when he finds out the truth? (Trap trilogy, #1)

Three's a Crowd

These romances each features a romantic triangle but not the triangles you learned about in high school geometry! These triangles are triads where all three partners are romantically and sexually involved.

Banks, Maya.
Brazen. 2007. Samhamien. ISBN 978159988146. 260pp.
   Scared and out of options, 16-year-old Jasmine is rescued by two brothers, Seth and Zane. Together they show her what it is like to be loved and cared for. Afraid of falling in love with one or both of them, she runs away to Paris. Coming back to them now, she is determined to make them see that she is all grown up and all the woman they need. Zane is all in from the beginning, having long had loved Jasmine from afar. Seth is not one to share anything, least of all his girlfriend. Jasmine is not giving up on both of them. For her, it is a two-for-one package deal.

Black, Shayla.
Ours to Love. 2013. Heat. ISBN 9780425253397. 389pp.
   Virginal London McLane was in a coma for two years following a horrific car accident that left her with years of surgery and pain. Doctors told her she would never walk, but she proved them wrong. The only lasting signs of her past are the occasional blackouts and the scars on her back. Getting on with her life, she has moved in with her cousin Alyssa and got a job working for Javier, who is more comfortable with a bottle of vodka than with other people. Thankfully Javier's brother Xander comes to help his brother and in the process meets the lovely London. Oh, the things the brothers want to do to her. Tired of living half a life, London is willing to see where this can take her. All she was looking for was someone to love her; now she has two men who will stop at nothing to love and protect her. (Wicked Lovers, #7)

Carew, Opal.
Twin Fantasies. 2007. St. Martin's Griffin. ISBN 9780312367787. 265pp.
   Sex with two men has been one of Jenna Kerry's most secret sexual fantasies. Too bad her fiancé Ryan doesn't share her fantasy. After backing out of attending a wedding reception with her, he decides to show up and gives her another one of her fantasies instead. Sex with a stranger. She goes along with it and has one night of wild, passionate sex. It turns out it wasn't Ryan but his twin brother Jake. Jenna seizes the opportunity to make her fantasy come true as the twins vie for her affection in the most erotic ways. What Jenna didn't plan on was falling in love with both of them.

Cunning, Olivia.
▶ *Double Time*. 2012. Sourcebooks Casablanca. ISBN 9781402271519. 406pp.

Reagan Elliot cannot believe her luck when she wins a contest to go on tour with her favorite rock band, Exodus End. Little does she know that along with the band comes guitarist Dare's brother Trey. Trey is bisexual but has just sworn off men when he meets Reagan. When Reagan goes on tour with Trey's band to learn the ropes, she and Trey cannot keep their hands off one another. While navigating a rough spot in their fledgling romance, Trey meets Ethan, Reagan's ex-boyfriend, current roommate. Trey's promise to swear off men is thrown out of the window as he struggles with his feelings for both Reagan and Ethan. When the three of them let their passions take them where they will, it is one encore worthy show. (Sinners on Tour, #3)

Dane, Lauren.
Tart. 2012. Berkley Trade. ISBN 9780425253250. 340pp.

Running the successful bakery Tart fills Juliet's days. She wishes she had her best friend Calvin to keep her busy at night, but even though they have known each other forever, he hasn't shown any interest in her. Moving on, she is more than happy when Gideon Carter, another childhood friend, comes back to town and begins to keep her nights more than busy. Calvin has always loved Jules, but he hasn't made a move on it but now seeing her with Gideon is too much. He wants her, and, to his surprise, Gideon too. The three bond in a highly sexual relationship that fulfills them all in every way. Second in the Delicious series.

Hart, Megan.
Tempted. 2012. Mira. ISBN 9780778315223. 426pp.

Anne and her husband James have a good life. They have a solid marriage. That all changes one summer when James's old friend Alex comes to town. Anne is very much attracted to Alex and he to her. When the tension gets to be too much to bear and the three have had too much wine, barriers are broken down and they share a night together like none they have ever experienced. Making a plan to enjoy each other for the summer, they embark on more nights like the first. At the end of the summer, this trio has developed strong feelings for one another and are rethinking their footloose and fancy-free plan of summer fun.

James, Lorelei.
Rough, Raw and Ready. 2009. Samhain. ISBN 9781605044040. 278pp.

Trevor Glanzer and Chassie West Glazner have been happily married for about a year, when an old friend and rodeo buddy of Trevor's comes by for a visit. Edgard is more than an old rodeo buddy, he and Trevor were lovers, and Edgard is eager to pick up where they left off. Trevor is torn between the man he once loved and the woman he loves now. Trevor has no intention of leaving Chassie but he still loves Edgard. As Trevor tries to sort it all out, Chassie and

Edgard slowly fall in love. This could be the perfect solution for Trevor. Maybe he can have it all. (<u>Rough Rider</u>, #5)

St. James, Jeanne.
  Double Dare. 2009. Loose ID. ISBN 9781607372936. 296pp.

Having sworn off men after being broken up with over e-mail, Quinn Preston is in no mood to attend a wedding. At the bar, she is drowning her sorrows in frothy drinks when she sees the very hot, very sexy Logan Reed. Her resolve goes out of the window as he takes her home with him, to sleep off her bender. No sex until she is sober. Soon enough she discovers that Logan is bisexual and in a committed relationship with Tyson White and ex-football player. What's a girl to do when faced with two hot guys? Snuggle down and enjoy them both! What starts out as an experiment on Quinn's part slowly ends up being so much more as the three of them find they are falling hard for one another.

Chapter Two

Character

Character is one of the strongest appeal factors for the romance novel. Readers are drawn to the books that they read because they identify in some way with the main character, or because the character is completely unlike themselves or anyone they know. Some readers seek out particular types of characters in their romances—firefighters, nerds, authors, African Americans. The characters' thought process and their feelings are the focal point in character-driven stories. The lists in this chapter bring together characters who are similar but who are experiencing very different things.

Shifty Characters

Shape-shifters are hot and feature prominently in romance. Though most are found in the modern world or the near future, shape-shifters are everywhere, including Regency England. For those looking for a little bit of a beast with their beauty, try one of these shape-shifter romances.

Bardsley, Michele.
Must Love Lycans. 2011. Signet. ISBN 9780451234506. 306pp.
What is the protocol for treating an amnesia patient who thinks he is a werewolf and is naked in your clinic? That's the task ahead of Kelsey as she starts her shift at the Dante Clinic. Trying to be professional about it while denying her very unprofessional thoughts are more difficult than Kelsey thought it would be. She discovers that werewolves really do exist and, after being accidentally bitten by Damien, waits to see if she will become one too. Damian

(her previously naked patient) is not only a werewolf but also the crown prince of werewolves. Giving up trying to deny her feelings for him leads to some seriously mind-blowing sex. Another solid entry into this funny paranormal series. (Broken Heart Vampires #8)

Cassidy, Dakota.
Accidental Werewolf. 2008. Berkley Trade. ISBN 9780425219300. 326pp.

While trying to break up a fight between her teacup poodle and a huge mutt, Marty is accidentally bitten. Her life as a sales rep for Bobbie Sue Cosmetics is going just fine; in fact, she just became Lavender on the color ladder of success. Now she is beginning to exhibit an alarming number of seemingly unrelated symptoms. There is also the problem of the incredibly hot and annoying neighbor Keegan, who insists that he is a werewolf. Only werewolves don't exist, do they? To protect and nurture Marty through the initial transition to becoming a werewolf, Keegan insists on bringing Marty to his family home. Be prepared to howl along in laughter and then fan yourself as the sparks between these two fly. (Accidental Friends, #1).

Dare, Lydia.
Certain Wolfish Charm. 2010. Sourcebooks Casablanca. ISBN 978140223 6945. 375pp.

The first in a trilogy focusing on a set of brothers with a secret. This first book introduces us to Simon, the Duke of Blackmore and legal guardian of Lily's nephew, Oliver. Oliver, her usually sweet and happy nephew, has suddenly become sullen, angry, and forever hungry. Desperate for answers and guidance, Lily travels to London for help from Simon. Once there, Simon takes over and helps with her nephew but won't tell Lily the real reason for her nephew's behavior . . . that he, like Simon and his brothers, is a werewolf. Despite the secret between them, there is a growing attraction that neither can ignore. Inevitably, things spiral out of control, and Lily finds herself compromised. The duke is not going to allow Lily's reputation to be tarnished and does the right thing by marrying her. Will he do the right thing and share his secret with her? A fun and steamy blend of paranormal and Regency romances. (Westfield Wolves, #1)

Harper, Molly.
How to Flirt with a Naked Werewolf. 2011. Pocket Books. ISBN 9781439195864. 371pp.

On the run from a broken engagement and her overbearing hippie parents, Mississippi native Mo Wenstein wasn't sure what to expect when she takes a job at the sole eatery in Grundy, Alaska. Finding herself attracted to rude, arrogant Cooper Graham certainly wasn't on the list. Cooper also happens to be a werewolf. Could he be the werewolf responsible for the recent vicious wolf attacks? Together Mo and Cooper generate enough heat to keep themselves warm during the cold Alaskan winter. It is a laugh-out-loud, lighthearted, but very sexy, romance. This is the first in a series featuring other members of Cooper's Were family. (Naked Werewolf, #1)

Harrison, Thea. ♛
Dragon Bound. 2011. Berkley Sensation. ISBN 9780425241509. 312pp.

Pia—half human and half Wyr—is on the run after being blackmailed into stealing something from Dragos Cuelebre, the most feared Wyr. He has caught her and is startled by his need to demand retribution and his overwhelming attraction to her. Dragos is used to getting what he wants and he wants Pia. As he tries to claim her and she fights back, the sex gets hotter and hotter. Their world of shifters, witches, fae, and goblins is on the brink of a major conflict. Can their romance survive? (Elder Races, #1)

Thompson, Vicki Lewis.
▶ *A Werewolf in Manhattan*. 2010. Signet. ISBN 9780451232472. 316pp.

Romance novelist Emma Gavin writes about werewolves using her imagination to supply the details about werewolf lore and lifestyle. Imagine her surprise when it appears that she is a bit too close to the truth. Aidan Wallace, the sexy security expert hired by her publisher to keep her safe on her book tour, is actually heir to the very wealthy, supersecretive werewolf pack in Manhattan. While trying to maintain a professional relationship, both of them realize that the attraction that runs between them is too strong to deny. Follow the further adventures of the Wallace pack in the next book, *Werewolf in the North Woods*. (Wild about You, #1)

Matchmaker, Matchmaker Make Me a Match

Sometimes you need a little help to find true love.

Bybee, Catherine.
Wife by Wednesday. 2013. CreateSpace. ISBN 978147964401. 244pp.

Blake Harrison needs a wife and he needs one now or by Wednesday, at the latest. His father has recently died, and if he's not married by his next birthday, his inheritance will pass to a cousin. A friend suggests he contact Sam Elliot, owner of Alliance, a matchmaking service. Sam turns out to be Samantha, a gorgeous redhead with a voice made for 900 numbers. Sam presents him with three choices, but Blake is determined to have her instead. With her younger sister in an expensive assisted living center, Sam can't afford to say no to $10 million for a one-year marriage in name only. Their marriage has to be convincing to the outside world, and as they spend more time together, the attraction between them grows. Will they both be able to walk away in a year, or is someone's heart going to get broken? (Weekday Brides, #1)

Dreiling, Vicky.
How to Marry a Duke. 2011. Forver. ISBN 9780446565370. 422pp.

Rule number one for any successful matchmaker is obvious—don't fall in love with your client. Sadly for Tessa, London's top matchmaker, she is about to break that rule trying to find a bride for one of her most challenging clients. Tessa tries to put her feelings for Tristan, Duke of Shelbourne, aside but as the contest she concocted to help him find a bride is coming to an end, she must confront her true feelings for the duke. She needs to find a way to do her job, see the contest through, maintain her sterling reputation with society, and convince the duke that she is the one he should be with. That's all in a day's work for this matchmaker. (How to, #1)

Guhrke, Laura Lee.
When the Marquess Met His Match. 2013. Avon. ISBN 9780062118172. 384pp.

Lady Belinda Featherstone married for love, but her husband made it perfectly clear to her that he was only in love with her money. When he died five years ago, he'd spent every last penny of her dowry. Determined that other young women not go through what she did, she becomes a matchmaker for other American heiresses. Nicholas Stirling, Marquess of Trubridge, is in need of a wealthy wife after his father cuts him off due to his scandalous behavior. At first she refuses to help him but then devises a plan to introduce him to several, completely unsuitable heiresses. The chemistry between them is intense, and as they get to know one another, they each find that there is more to the other than they first thought. Belinda is feisty and flawed, while Nicholas is charming and misunderstood. (American Heiress in London, #1)

Kelley, Christie.
One Night Scandal. 2011. Zebra. ISBN 9781420108781. 352pp.

As the illegitimate daughter of an earl, Sophie Reynard's place in society is somewhat precarious, and she has few marriage prospects. Sophie has psychic abilities and has used them in the past to match up her society friends. While visiting Venice, she falls off a bridge and into a canal. She is rescued by "Nico," and when a vision tells her that he is the one, she spends one amazing night with him. Then she learns that he is Nicholas Tenbury, Marquess of Ancroft, and knows that due to the circumstances of her birth, they cannot be together. Nicholas can't stop thinking about her, and when he returns to London, his friends encourage him to visit Miss Reynard to find his match. A lot of back and forth ensues, as Sophie believes that she will ruin his life, and Nicolas persists in being with her. Engaging characters and spicy sex scenes add up to a solid historical romance. (Spinsters Club, #5)

Norfleet, Celeste O.
One Sure Thing. 2002. Harlequin Kimani. ISBN 9781583144039. 320pp.

Mamma Lou is determined to match up and marry off her bachelor grandson, Dr. Raymond Gates. Raymond says he's a hopeless case and challenges Mamma Lou to find him hope. After overhearing a conversation in the ladies room while at the theater, that's exactly what she does. After finding out more about emergency room doctor, Hope Adams, Mamma Lou uses her almond allergy to arrange meetings between Hope and Raymond. Hope's mother was killed by her stepfather, and her own prior relationships have left her distrusting men and vowing not to get into another relationship, but Raymond is determined to get past her issues and have more Hope in his life. (Mamma Lou Matchmaker, #3).

Phillips, Susan Elizabeth.
▶ *Match Me If You Can*. 2005. Avon. ISBN 9780060734565. 388pp.
　　In a family of overachievers, Annabelle Granger stands out and not in a good way. At 31 years old, she's had several failed careers and a failed engagement. When her grandmother dies, Annabelle inherits Matches by Myrna and her elderly clients. She renames the business Perfect for You and sets out to find a high-profile client. She gets an introduction to Heath Champion, a leading sports agent, and even though Heath has signed a contract with the leading Chicago matchmaking firm, Power Matches, he agrees to let Annabelle set him up on one date. Heath is a self-made man with a trailer park past and is determined to find the perfect society wife. Annabelle is a delightful heroine, not at all what Heath is looking for in a wife and yet, somehow she's perfect for him, but they go through a lot to get there. Many of the secondary characters are from previous books, but Phillips also introduces some new characters who get their own stories in later books. (Chicago Stars, #6)

Springer, Kristina.
The Espressologist. 2009. Farrar, Strauss and Giroux. ISBN 9780374322281. 184pp. [Y][A]
　　Jane Turner is a 17-year-old barista at a popular coffee chain. She keeps track of what types of coffee drinks people order and believes their coffee preferences are a good indicator of what kind of person they are. When a regular customer comes in after a breakup, Jane sets him up with another customer. News of her matchmaking spreads, and her boss offers up her services as a holiday promotion. It takes a little longer for Jane to make her own match, but readers will enjoy this light, frothy teen romance. Make that an iced mocha latte for me!

Nerds in Love

Maybe we have it all wrong and it is really the nerds who, underneath it all, are the true superheroes.

MacAlister, Katie.
Blow Me Down. 2005. Signet. ISBN 9780451216397. 359pp.
　　Earless Erika (aka Amy) and Black Corbin meet on the high seas of "Buckling Swashes," a virtual reality game. Little does Amy know that besides

being one very sexy pirate, Black Corbin is really the game's creator. Soon enough, Amy and Corbin realize they are trapped in the virtual world. High jinks and love on the high seas ensue as they work together to free themselves and save the game from destruction.

McReynolds, Glenna.
River of Eden. 2002. Random House. ISBN 9780553583939. 352pp.

Dr. Annie Parrish is trying to recover from the infamous Woolly Monkey incident by finding a rare orchid deep in the Amazon rainforest. To do that, she needs the help of Will Travers. He's a Harvard-educated scientist who has turned his back on the scientific community, choosing instead to spend his days ferrying people up and down the Amazon. Adventure, intrigue, and romance abound as they try to stay one step ahead of the slew of people who want one or both of them dead for a variety of reasons.

▶ **Miller, Leah Rae.**
The Summer I Became a Nerd. 2013. Entangled Publishing. ISBN 978162 0612385. 258pp.

Maddie is torn. Not between two lovers, well not yet, but she is torn between the two sides of herself: popular cheerleader and comic book–loving nerd. By day Maddie is a cheerleader, all around popular senior, even dating the cute but boring quarterback of the football team, but by night she's a comic book–reading, anime-watching nerd. This summer is the summer that changes all that and forces Maddie to come to terms with her two sides. It is also the summer that forces her to decide between cute but boring Eric and the "adorkable" Logan, who works at the Phoenix comic shop and hosts his own late night radio show. Nerds unite in this fun summer romance.

Monroe, Lucy.
The Real Deal. 2004. Kensington. ISBN 9780758208606. 352pp.

Amanda is still reeling emotionally from her divorce several years ago. Living for her work, she is a corporate negotiator eager to close the deal between her company and a small family-owned computer company. The deal hinges on convincing computer genius drop-dead sexy Simon that the deal is a good thing. The problem is that Simon drifts off in pursuit of his latest thought right in the middle of Amanda's presentation. To cinch the deal, she does what any sensible business person would do . . . she moves into his home so she can meet with him whenever he is available. Amanda tries to stay focused on business but Simon is so distracting. This is one case where business and pleasure do mix.

Roberts, Nora.
Vision in White. 2009. Berkley Trade. ISBN 9780425227510. 343pp.

Mackensie prefers to be behind the scenes, photographing the weddings that she plans with her three best girlfriends at Vows, their full-service wedding-planning business. A bit of a workaholic, she's not really looking for marriage and then she meets geeky English teacher, Carter Maguire. He's about to teach her that there's more to life than work. Good thing he is patient because Mackensie is his toughest student yet. (Bride Quartet, #1)

Thompson, Vicki Lewis.
Nerd in Shining Armor. 2003. Dell. ISBN 9780440241164. 324pp.

Who says playing videogames is a waste of time? Nerdy computer programmer Jack Farley's flight simulator game skills saved his life and Genevieve's life. Crash landing a plane on a remote island, Jack managed to foil their boss Nick's plan to kill them both, this time. Alone on a remote island with the woman that he has been secretly in love with, Jack is out to prove that he is the hero that Genevieve now thinks he is. (Nerds, #1)

Uniformly Hot

What is it about men in uniform? Is it the authority they command, or is it just that no matter how hot they look in the uniform, that we are just as eager to see what lies underneath the uniform?

Blake, Toni.
Sugar Creek. 2010. Avon. ISBN 9780061765797. 384pp.

Rachel Farris is heading home to help her grandmother out with the harvest at the family apple orchard in Destiny, Ohio. She hoped for a quick trip. Just long enough to help with the apples, visit with her old girlfriends and then head home. No fuss, no muss. She barely makes it into Destiny when the trouble starts. That Romo clan is going to be the death of her. A longstanding feud between their family and hers is the undercurrent for hot and sexy Officer Mike Romo's penchant for giving Rachel parking tickets. With tensions running high, Rachel and Mike discover that feuding isn't nearly as much fun as making up. (Destiny, #2)

Brockmann, Suzanne.
▶ *Born to Darkness*. 2012. Ballantine. 9780345521286. 595pp.

Former navy SEAL Shane Laughlin finally landed a job at the Obermeyer Institute (OI) in this dark near-future thriller. The night before he goes up to the OI, he has one night of amazing sex with Michelle "Mac" Mackenzie. Shane can't believe it when he shows up for work and sees Mac there. She's a "Greater Than" someone who has superior brain powers and special abilities. The OI's current mission is to fight against the organization making a new drug called Destiny. Destiny is incredibly addictive and expensive, but it allows non–Greater Thans to experience what it feels like to be a Greater Than. Working as team, Shane and Mac are a train wreck of fighting, misunderstanding, and failed communications, but in the bedroom, they are all sparks, fireworks, and pleasure. A romance between secondary characters Stephen Diaz, also a Greater Than, and Dr. Elliot Zerkowisk, a researcher at the OI, unfolds as well. First in the <u>Fighting Destiny</u> series.

Buchman, M.L.
Take over at Midnight. 2013. Sourcebooks. ISBN 9781402258190. 370pp.

Being a helicopter pilot was something that Lola LaRue has wanted to do forever. She makes it and joins a Special Operations Aviation Regiment (SOAR) team in Pakistan. She is a long way from the brothel she was raised in. Because of her unconventional upbringing, she doesn't trust people, especially men or believe in relationships. Sergeant Tim Maloney is determined to change that. For him it was love at first sight. Over the course of one dangerous assignment after another, he slowly befriends Lola and works his way into her heart. (<u>Night Stalkers</u>, #4.)

Donovan, Susan.
I Want Candy. 2012. St. Martins. 9780312536220. 352pp.

After losing everything in a series of bad business decisions, Candy comes home ashamed and wanting nothing more than to hide out until she can figure out how to get back on her feet again. What she didn't count on was her attraction to the very handsome and sexy Sheriff Turner. Add in a crazy militia group who might or might not be responsible for his wife's death and a demented stalker, and it is all Turner can do to protect and keep Candy safe. Candy is trying not to fall for Turner because she isn't planning on staying put, but a man in uniform is hard to resist. Donovan's blend of small-town charm, humor, and sexy romance is a sure hit! (<u>Bigler, North Carolina</u>, #2)

Essex, Elizabeth.
Almost a Scandal. 2012. St. Martins. ISBN 9781250003799. 368pp.

To save their family's pride and place within society, Sally Kent does the unthinkable. When her brother doesn't show up to do his service with the British Royal Navy, she dons his clothing and steps aboard the *Audacious* in his stead. Having grown up on water, she proves herself to be a valuable member of the crew. Working hard to keep her secret, she is hindered by one thing . . . the commander of the ship is none other than Lieutenant David Colyear, a family friend whom Sally has been infatuated with for years. Not surprisingly, he discovers her secret, but he has no choice but to keep it to himself. In the midst of battle and danger, he realizes that he has very strong feelings for her. They mustn't act on them though. To the rest of the crew, Sally is a man, and during the Napoleonic Wars, relations between two men were simply not tolerated. When their tour of duty is over, will they be free to act upon their feelings, or will they be forced to continue the charade Sally began? (<u>Reckless Brides</u>, #1)

Fredrick, M. J.
Don't Look Back. 2010. Wild Rose Press. ISBN 9781601547972. 254pp.

Seven years ago, Dr. Olivia "Liv" Olney was captured, tortured, raped, and beaten half to death in Africa. She was rescued by Captain Gerard "Del" Delany. It has taken her a long time to put her life back together again but she has. She is devastated when her best friend Jill is taken hostage by the same man who took her. With no one else to turn to, she calls on Del to help her. He has spent the last few years in exile in Spain due to a mission gone bad, but how can he turn his back on Liv? Together they go to Africa to try and find Jill. While fighting horrible enemies, monsoons, and other horrors, they find it in their hearts to give love a chance. An inspiring look at love after a tragedy combined with seriously hot and sizzling romance!

Leigh, Lora.
Wild Card. 2008. St. Martins. ISBN 9780739498583. 417pp.

A new series by Leigh that is a spin-off of her popular <u>Tempting SEALs</u> series. Nathan was a Navy SEAL. His mission was supposed to be simple—infiltrate a drug cartel in Colombia, secure the captives, and get the hell out of there. It didn't quite go down that way. Nathan was captured and held captive for 18 months—18 long months full of torture and pain. When he finally escapes, he is a shell of the man he used to be. A shell of the man that Bella was married to. He lets her believe that he is dead and assumes another identity to save her from being with the monster he believes he has turned into. Now working with an elite operations team as Noah, he comes back into contact with Bella. Bella is not the same woman she was when they were married. When her business comes under attack, Noah is there to save her. By saving her life, he finds a way to let her back into his heart and life again. (<u>Elite Ops</u>, #1)

Melton, Marliss.
In the Dark. 2005. Forever. ISBN 9780446614924. 336pp.

Kidnapped and held captive in a Cuban Jail, Defense Intelligence agent Hannah Geary is a woman looking for revenge. Not just for her but for her partner who was killed in the line of duty as well. Lieutenant Luther Lindstrom rescued Hannah and he and his team are helping build a case against the rogue SEAL commander who betrayed her. Lovitt is about to get his due. Luther agrees to protect and keep Hannah safe. He is attracted to her, but he just ended a relationship, and now is looking for a woman who will be happy to stay home and be a wife. He is looking for someone who won't be influenced by his former NFL football player status. Hannah just wants to be in the field working with the CIA. She knows that Luther is the man for her but can they overcome their different ideas of domestic life? In the end, they both want the same thing—to love and to be loved. Action packed and full of twists and turns, keeping you guessing until the very end. (<u>Navy SEAL Team 12</u>, #2). This book is dedicated to Pat Tilman, former NFL player–turned–Army ranger.

Come on Baby, Light My Fire

Doesn't every girl have fantasies of being rescued by a hunky firefighter?

Anderson, Susan.
  Burning Up. 2010. Harlequin. ISBN 9780373774982. 376pp.
      Having left tiny Sugarville, Washington, 10 years ago in shame and scandal, Macy O'James never intended to come back. She only comes back to help care for her injured cousin. In the years since she left town, she has become famous for her sexy music videos. Returning home isn't going to be easy, but Macy is determined to do it and to do it proudly. She didn't count of meeting the irresistible fire chief Gabriel Donovan at her family's boarding house. New in town, Gabriel has heard all about Macy and the scandal that went down. All the gossip in the world doesn't change the intense attraction between them. While navigating the waters of their fledgling relationship, Macy has to come to terms with an old enemy, and Gabriel has to decide if he can handle the flamboyant creature who sets his heart aflame.

Andre, Bella.
  Never Too Hot. 2010. Bantam. ISBN 9780440245025. 368pp.
      Ginger Sinclair has spent the past months at a secluded cabin in the Adirondacks recovering from an abusive marriage and finding herself. Connor MacKenzie, ex-firefighter, has left California and his Hot Shot crew behind after he was scarred badly in a fire he couldn't outrun. He heads home to the family cabin to lick his wounds and to train so that if and when the crew says he can come back he is ready. He didn't expect to find anyone at the cabin, let alone the beautiful artist he discovers in his living room. The two come to terms and agree to share the house. It isn't long before they are sharing more than that as the two wounded souls begin to heal one another. A secondary romance is also told about Connor's father Andrew and the lost love of his life, Isabel. (Hot Shots, #3)

Bernard, Jennifer.
  ▶ *The Fireman Who Loved Me*. 2012. Avon. ISBN 9780062088963. 384pp.
      The first book in the Bachelor Fireman of San Gabriel is a red hot romance! News producer Melissa McGuire leaves Los Angeles for San Gabriel after a relationship gone wrong. She moves in with her grandmother, Nelly, who is determined to find her a husband. Without telling Melissa, Nelly bids on a date with a fireman at a bachelor auction for her, but a curse on the firehouse dooms all of the firemen to be unlucky in love. Neither Melissa nor Harry is looking for a relationship, but the sparks seem to fly whenever they're together. Can they break the curse? Bernard's debut is a light humorous romance with delightful secondary characters. (The Bachelor Firemen of San Gabriel, #1)

Davis, Jo.
Line of Fire. 2010. Signet. ISBN 9780451229786. 320pp.

   Twenty-three-year-old firefighter Tommy Skyler is at a crossroads in his young life. Having quit playing football before he made it into the NFL, he is not sure firefighting is where he wants to be. Lately he has been thinking about moving into arson investigation. He might not be sure of his career path, but he is sure that his future involves emergency room (ER) nurse Shea Ford. Shea's not so sure. She's a few years older than Tommy and is afraid of being burned like she has been in the past. After an injury lands Tommy in her ER, she can't help but say yes to a date. While they explore their new relationship, Tommy has his work cut out for him. There is a rash of arson fires that Tommy is determined to get to the bottom of. In spite of the danger, their love blossoms in this steamy and suspenseful romance. This is the fourth book in the Fire Fighters of Station Five series. Readers are treated to visits from all the characters from the previous books. This can, however, be read as a stand-alone.

Marsh, Anne.
Burning Up. 2012. Brava. ISBN 9780758266811. 277pp.

   Jack is a smoke jumper; he goes where the fires are—until the summer that his Nonna asked him to come home and watch out for one of his hometown's girls. Someone is stalking Lily, Jack's old high school sweetheart. Jack and his team of smoke jumpers are determined to keep Lily safe. Jack is determined to finish what they started in high school, and despite Lily's reluctance, the passion building between them is hot enough to start a few wildfires of their own.

Shay, Kathryn.
After the Fire. 2003. Berkley. ISBN 9780425193044. 384pp.

   After a tragic fire, three firefighting siblings vow to change their lives for the better. Jenn wants to have a baby and asks her best friend, roommate, and fellow firefighter, Grady, to be a sperm-donor. Mitch wants to resolve things once and for all with his wife Connie and be a better father to his teenage children but finds himself falling for the new police detective, Megan Hale. Zach just wants to get his life back on track. A compelling novel about family with lots of action, realistic details about firefighting, and several short, but intense, sex scenes. Read more about the Malveso family in *On the Line*.

The Spy Who Loved Me

Mystery, danger, romance, betrayal, passion, international intrigue? We got that!

Abramson, Traci Hunter.
Royal Target. 2008. Covenant Communications, Inc. ISBN 9781598116282. 257pp.

   Janessa Rogers, a beautiful young CIA operative, is assigned to protect the royal family of Meridia. She expects to do this using her language and security skills, not by getting engaged to the younger son, Prince Garrett Fortier. Janessa finds herself falling for the prince but can't let it get in the way of her ability to do the job; she also can't consider a serious relationship with someone from another faith if she wants to have a temple marriage. Garrett falls for her as well and, unbeknownst to Janessa, has been investigating the LDS church for years. Abramson's personal experience working for the CIA comes through and adds realism to an unlikely Cinderella story.

Carter, Ally.
I'd Tell You I Love You, but Then I'd Have to Kill You. 2006. Disney-Hyperion. ISBN 9781423100034. 288pp. ⓎⒶ
    Cammie Morgan is a student at the elite Gallagher Academy for Exceptional Young Women. The Virginia school is actually a school for CIA spies in training. While on a mission for one of her classes, she meets Josh Abrams, a normal teenage boy. They start dating, and Cammie soon realizes that being a girl can be more difficult than training to be a spy. She can't tell Josh where she goes to school, and one lie leads to another. Cute characters, a fast-paced plot, and funny dialogue make this teen romance a great escape. (Gallagher Girl, #1)

Cornwall, Lecia.
The Secret Life of Lady Julia. 2013. Avon. ISBN 9780062202451. 384pp.
    Julia Leighton was betrothed to the Duke of Temberlay at an early age. At her engagement ball, she meets Thomas Merritt, a jewel thief, who was there to steal her mother's tiara. A steamy encounter between them in her father's library leaves her pregnant; her family disowns her and insists that she leave the country. Julia gets a position as a paid companion to Dorothea Hallam, the widowed sister of diplomat Major Lord Stephen Ives. They travel to Vienna for the peace conference following Napoleon's imprisonment on Elba, and Julia's language skills are put to use. Then in Vienna, she meets up with Thomas again. Cornwall delivers a fast-paced tale of political intrigue with an unconventional hero and heroine who interact with many historical figures of the time.

Galen, Shana.
Lord and Lady Spy. 2011. Sourcebooks, Inc. ISBN 9781402259074. 376pp.
    Lord Adrian Smythe and his wife Sophia have a marriage of convenience. With the Napoleonic Wars raging, the two have spent very little time together. This has worked out well for Sophia, as she has been keeping quiet about her secret life as a spy known as the Saint. What she doesn't know is that Adrian, the Wolf, has also been working for the elite Barbican group. When Napoleon is captured, they are both told that their services are no longer required. When a new assignment becomes available, they are each called back, but only one of them will get a permanent assignment. As they discover more about each other and themselves, sparks fly. An interesting take on the Regency romance

with lots of intrigue, witty dialogue, competitive spirit, and passion. (Lord and Lady Spy, #1)

Quick, Amanda.
The Mystery Woman. 2013. Putnam. ISBN 9780399159091. 357pp.

Beatrice Lockwood, aka Miranda the Clairvoyant, has been using her psychic abilities to support herself. When her employer is killed, she winds up on Lantern Street working for the Marsh Agency, protecting a debutante from a fortune hunter. In this capacity, she meets Joshua Gage, a former spy for the Crown, who is recovering from injuries. Joshua initially believes that Beatrice has been blackmailing his sister; he quickly realizes that she is not the blackmailer and the two team up to investigate. This brings them into contact with a mad scientist, who believes that Beatrice is the key to resurrecting his dead love, who he has been keeping in a crystal sarcophagus. The second in the Ladies of Lantern Street series is a smart, fast-paced tale that will keep readers on the edge of their seats and their lights on until dawn, as they read on to find out what happens next.

Randol, Anna.
Sins of a Wicked Princess. 2013. Avon. ISN 9780062231406. 384pp.

Ian Maddox, the Wraith, is one of the Trio, a top secret group of English spies that was disbanded after Napoleon's death. When he discovers that someone is trying to kill the three of them, he is determined to track them down and use the skills that he learned after being recruited from the gallows to eliminate the threat. All the clues point to Princess Julianna Castanova. Julianna had to leave her homeland of Lenoria after a rebellion caused by the Trio led to the death of her parents. Julianna offers her help in finding out who is trying to kill him if he will help her regain her kingdom. The third book in the Wickedly Tempting series offers plenty of steamy stolen moments and intrigue. Can a princess and a spy overcome their social differences and find a happy ending?

Robinson, Gina.
Live and Let Love. 2013. St. Martin's Press. ISBN 978031252412. 325pp.

Secret Agent Jack Pierce nearly died two years ago when the Revolutionary International Organization of Terrorists (RIOT) tried to take him out. Only a handful of people know that he's still alive, and after having reconstructive surgery to fix the damage caused by the explosion, Jack is unrecognizable. The catch? Shane Kennet, aka "The Rooster," is romancing his widow, Willow. In the two years since Jack died, Willow has tried to move on. To escape the memories, she has moved across the state and pursued her dream of opening her own candy store. Jack's boss at the National Clandestine Service offers him the chance to get revenge by killing the man who was sent to kill him. When Willow meets her next-door neighbor's cousin Con Russo, she's sure that he's really Jack. Jack can't give up his cover while the safety of the country is at stake, but Willow is a temptation that is hard to resist. Robinson's humorous sexy tale is the third in the <u>Agent Ex</u> series.

Stuart, Anne.
▶ *Black Ice*. 2005. Mira. ISBN 9780778321712. 377pp.

Chloe Underwood is an American in Paris. She comes from a family of doctors but has resisted their efforts to get her to go to medical school; instead, she translates children's books. Hoping for a little more action and adventure in her life and looking to supplement her slight income, Chloe jumps at the chance to fill in for her roommate as a translator for a group of businessmen. Arriving at the Chateau where they are spending the weekend, she gets a bad feeling but decides to stick it out. It turns out the businessmen are arms dealers. Bastien Toussaint works for the committee and has spent the last two years infiltrating the cartel. Chloe's innocence is a great foil for Bastien's dark side, and she has some great lines. This one is not for the squeamish—the sex is hot and the violence can be graphic, but the romance makes it worth it. Put it at the top of your to-be-read pile, we guarantee you won't be sorry! (<u>Ice</u>, #1)

Signed, Sealed, Delivered, I'm Yours: Mail-Order Brides and Grooms

These brave women left behind their families and homes and everything familiar to them for a variety of reasons and journeyed a long distance hoping to find a better life and love.

Bliss, Lauralee.
Love Finds You in Bethlehem, New Hampshire. 2009. Summerside Press. ISBN 978193541620. 295pp.

Up-and-coming artist Thomas Haskins has been advised by his mentor that he should begin to seriously think about taking a bride. Having seen the success of other mail-order bride marriages, he placed an ad in a New York City paper. He has a vision of an educated, proper, God-fearing woman that will take her dutiful place by his side in the picturesque town of Bethlehem, New Hampshire. Penniless and living on the streets, Sara McGee replies and soon finds herself on a train to New Hampshire. Upon first sight, Thomas realizes this was a mistake. Sara is not refined, educated, or anything close to his vision. She must go back. Luckily, Thomas' sister Claire has come home to act as a chaperone and takes Sara under wing. Claire educates Sara in the art of becoming a lady. While she is learning how to be a lady, and falling in love with the gentle Thomas, another lady has caught the attention of Thomas. After all that Sara has been through, is she going to lose Thomas to another woman? It takes a few misunderstandings and a return trip to New York for Thomas to see that Sara really is the woman that he wants as his wife. Educated, not educated, refined or not, he loves Sara. Part of the <u>Love Finds You</u> series.

Brendan, Maggie.
Twice Promised. 2012. Revell. ISBN 978080073463. 336pp.

Jess Gifford, owner of a general store in Central City, Colorado, has no idea what is about to erupt. His younger brother Zack has taken the liberty of placing an ad for a mail-order bride for Jess. It seems that Zack wants out of working at the mercantile and he thinks that a wife might help the very disorganized Jess get organized. Imagine Jess's surprise when not one but two would-be brides arrive at his store. Zack thoughtfully narrowed the selection down to two and is leaving the final pick to Jess. Bride-to-be number one, Greta Olsen saw how well her sister's mail-order marriage worked, and after the death of her fiancé, she is ready to move on. Bride number two Cora Johnson was living at home but was more than ready to escape from under her parents' roof. Jess is going to have to make a choice but not before getting to know both women and some hilarious misunderstandings.

Cabot, Amanda.
Paper Roses. 2009. Revell. ISBN 9780800733247. 378pp.

Sarah Dobbs and her young sister Thea have just stepped off the train in San Antonio. They have come from Philadelphia so that Sarah could start a new life as a mail-order bride. Her intended groom, whose letters were so endearing that Sarah treasures them, is nowhere to be found. Instead, his brother Clay arrives to pick Sarah up with the terrible news that Austin is dead. With no place to go, Sarah and Thea head to the family ranch to stay with Clay and his father, Robert. Clay is bent on finding out who shot and killed Austin, while Sarah takes on the mission of educating the town's children. As they are building separate lives within the same household, Sarah and Clay begin to first develop a friendship and then a romantic relationship. They struggle with issues of forgiveness and anger, but they weather those storms together. (<u>Texas Dreams</u> #1)

Fresina, Jayne.
The Most Improper Miss Sophie Valentine. 2012. Sourcebooks. ISBN 978140 2265976. 375pp.

Sophie Valentine, aged 30, is on the shelf and tired of living with her brother and his family. She has decided it is time to get married and, in true Sophie fashion, does it her way. She scandalizes the family by advertising for a husband in the *Farmers Gazette*. Lazarus Kane answers her ad. He has been enamored of Sophie since he saw her leaping out of a building to escape marriage years earlier. Not quite the husband material that Sophie's brother was hoping for, he tries to convince Sophie to marry her old beau (the one she jumped off the balcony to avoid marrying). A delightful twist on the arranged marriage trope.

Johnston, Joan.
Texas Bride. 2012. Random House. ISBN 9780345527448. 384pp.

Each hiding something from the other, Jake Creed and Miranda Wentworth enter into a marriage based on a mail-order bride advertisement Jake placed. Miranda is desperate to find a home for herself and her two younger brothers to save them from a cruel master at the orphanage and is hopeful that later she can bring her other siblings to her new home. Jake is in need of a mother for his young daughter, whose mother died in childbirth. He is haunted by the idea of loving another woman only to lose her too. He planned to marry Miranda in name only. Finding his new bride fitting so well into his family and life, he can't help but fall in love with her. Can he overcome his fear and let her into his bed as well as his heart?

Landis, Jill Marie.
Summer Moon. 2002. Ballantine Books. ISBN 9780345440396. 416pp.

Answering an ad for a mail-order bride Kate Whittington thought was the answer to her prayers. The orphanage where she was raised and later taught was being shut down and she had no job and place to live. Becoming a mail-order bride seemed like the best answer to both problems. If it were only that easy. After exchanging letters, she agreed to marry Reed Benton by proxy. When she arrives in Texas, she discovers that Reed Sr. has died and the ad was really placed for his son, Reed Jr. Reed Jr had no idea about this and wants nothing to do with a mail-order bride. He has enough to deal with now that he has been injured in a fight with the Comanche and has brought back a boy, Daniel, who he is convinced is his son captured by the Comanche when they raided the village and killed his wife. Kate takes a liking to Daniel but isn't entirely sure that this is the place for her. It takes Daniel running away and Kate and Reed teaming up to find him to show her that her place is right there in Texas with Reed and Daniel.

Lowe, Fiona. ♛
Boomerang Bride. 2012. Carina Press. ISBN 9780373002054. 352pp.

When Marc Olson arrives in Hobin, Wisconsin, for his annual Thanksgiving visit, he is surprised to find a bride, complete with a wedding cake, standing in front of a shop on Main Street. Matilda Geoffrey quit her job and flew from Australia to Wisconsin to surprise her fiancé; however, the surprise in on her—no one knows Barry and their joint savings account is empty. Matilda settles into the small community, finding two temporary jobs while she figures out what to do with her life. Marc just wants to get this vacation over with and return home, but there is something about Matilda that he finds so appealing. Filled with humor and pathos, the characters have substance and depth. Matilda is spunky, smart, and vulnerable; Marc is emotionally stunted; he has made a lot of sacrifices for his family and is afraid of having to give up his dreams. A secondary story involving Marc's sisters' breast cancer surgery and the aftermath is exceptionally well handled.

Warner, Kaki.
Heartbreak Creek. 2011. Berkeley Trade. ISBN 9780425241226. 384pp.

Widowed Edwina Ladoux answers widower Declan Brodie's ad for a mail-order bride to help on the ranch and to raise his four children in the wilds of Colorado. Declan had specified in his ad for a "sturdy woman," not a southern belle. Having already been married by proxy, they give themselves three months to see if the arrangement will work before having the marriage annulled. With her half-sister Prudence's help, Edwina sets about to learning how to be a rancher's wife and a stepmother. Threats of violence from neighboring Indians, out-of-control children, and a completely unfamiliar landscape almost have Edwina running for the annulment but as the weeks pass, she begins to calm the children, deal with the different landscape, and sees her husband in a new light. It takes a surprise from Declan's past to make him see that his future and that of his family rest with Edwina. A gently developing romance. (Runaway Brides, #1)

Love Me, Love My Dog

Men may act like dogs sometimes, but in these romances the dogs may steal your heart.

Cates, Kimberly.
▶ *Perfect Match*. 2007. Harlequin. ISBN 9780373772650. 379pp.

Rowena Brown has a talent for matching people with pets. She moves from Chicago to tiny Whitewater, Illinois, to open up a pet store after her Aunt Maeve tells her that she'll find her soul mate there. Rowena runs into trouble with the law from the start. Her Newfoundland Clancy, aka Destroyer, has practically demolished the tea shop next door and Deputy Cash Lawless wants him put down. Rowena rescues Clancy and finds his perfect match; unfortunately, for everyone involved she is Cash's daughter Charlie. Cash has his hands full raising Charlie and her sister Mac, who is in a wheelchair. This one has a little bit of everything—a heartwarming story that will bring you to tears, characters that are fully developed, sweet and spicy sex, a touch of magic, and a dog that steals the show.

Donovan, Susan.
Ain't Too Proud to Beg. 2009. St. Martin's Paperbacks. ISBN 9780312366049. 352pp.

Thirty-five-year-old obituary writer Josie Sheehan has had 11 boyfriends since college, and her only long-term relationship with a male is with her Labradoodle, Genghis. Josie and her three dog-walking friends have all sworn off men. While doing an interview with an elderly widow, the woman suggests that she puts what she wants in writing. Soon after, she meets Rick Rousseau, the CEO of a pet company. Josie and Rick hit it off, but Rick comes with a lot of baggage—serious baggage. Rick's last girlfriend recently died; she was in a coma for seven years after he caused a motorcycle accident and he hasn't had sex since. A wacky romantic comedy with serious elements and really hot sex, *Beg* is the first in the Dog Walkers trilogy. (Dog Walkers, #1).

Fox, Elaine.
Beware of Doug. 2007. Avon. ISBN 9780061739019. 384pp.

College professor Lily Tyler is in love with the perfect man Gerald, who is one of the lawyers in her father's firm. Even Doug, her so-ugly-he's-cute French bulldog likes him, but Gerald seems content to end their dates with a chaste kiss on the cheek. Pilot Brady Cole moves into the other half of Lily's duplex. He broke one too many hearts in DC, and after getting involved with a woman who starts stalking him, he goes on a "date diet." Lily and Brady are attracted to each other, but Brady can't seem to make friends with man's best friend, and that's a deal breaker. The second entry in Fox's Guys and Dogs series is LOL funny, but you must love dogs.

Graves. Jane.
Stray Hearts. 2013. Jane Graves. ISBN 9780988344129. 161pp.

When Kay Ramsey catches her fiancé cheating on her, she does what any woman would do. She hires a dog-grooming service to shave Up You (it was supposed to be Up Yours, but they ran out of dog) into the coat of his prize-winning cocker spaniels. Robert sues her and, when he wins, tells her that he'll forget the money that she owes him if she does 100 hours of community service at a local animal shelter. No problem, except that Kay is terrified of animals. Dr. Matt Foster can't turn down an animal in need but is barely making enough to keep the doors of his shelter open. Robert offers to make sure that he wins a grant, but only if he makes Kay's time at the shelter miserable. Matt is instantly attracted to Kay, but after his divorce, he has no plans to get involved with another woman, especially an animal hater. Kay can't help but notice Matt, but there's no way she could fall for a vet. Will Kay be able to conquer her fears and find true love? A quick, cute read with adorable animals.

Martin, Deidre.
Chasing Stanley. 2007. Berkley. ISN: 9780425214473. 345pp.

When professional hockey player Jason Mitchell is traded to his favorite hockey team, the New York Blades, he couldn't be happier. He's spent most of his life living in the middle of nowhere, so he's excited to sample everything the city has to offer. Stanley, Jason's Newfoundland isn't exactly suited to city life, and when Jason meets dog trainer Delilah Gould, he thinks his problems are over. Jason and Delilah couldn't be more different, but something (besides Stanley) draws them together. Their differences create a lot of conflict, but if they can't learn to accept each other for who they are, they may not be able to make their relationship work. Although this is a light romance, Martin covers some serious issues, including religious differences, sibling rivalry, and dysfunctional families. (New York Blades, #5)

Watson, Elsa.
The Love Dog. 2013. Tor. ISBN 9780765368096. 336pp.

    Fired from her job as a paralegal and up to her ears in debt, Sam reluctantly takes a job writing for a tabloid magazine. Her first assignment is a series of exposé articles on the wildly popular TV reality show *The Love Dog*. At first she is more than happy to expose the dark side of the show but soon she falls in love not just with Apollo, the Love Dog, but with Mason, the show's handsome host. When her betrayal of the show threatens to destroy their blossoming relationship, Sam is holding out hope that Apollo will work his magic and keep their love alive.

Lawyers in Love

    Lawyers are known for their competitive, aggressive natures. These titles put those traits to the test both in the courtroom and the bedroom.

Deveraux, Jude.
Stranger in the Moonlight. 2012. Pocket Books. ISBN 9781416509752. 362pp.

    As children, Kim, 8, and Travis, 12, meet when Travis arrives in Edilean, Virginia, for two wonderful weeks, where they play, ride bikes, and have the time of their life. Then Travis disappears with no warning and no goodbye. Before he left, he told her that he would someday return for her. The dreamer in Kim has held on to that promise for almost 20 years, carrying a photo of she and Travis with her as one of her most cherished possessions. She has stayed in Edilean, creating a life for herself complete with a business of her own—making jewelry—and a boyfriend. He's not what she has imagined Travis might have grown into, but he is okay. Travis has spent his life trying to become the man he thinks Kim deserves. Now a successful lawyer in New York, he travels back to Edilean for his mother's wedding and to convince Kim that he is the one for her. Can their adult selves measure up to their childhood dreams and fantasies?

Gabrielle, Tina.
In the Barrister's Bed. 2010. Zebra Books. ISBN 9781420122756. 344pp.

    Wydmoor Manor, the ancestral home of the Duke of Blackwood, was sold when the duke died without a legitimate heir. Widow Bella Sinclair bought the home just three days before James Devlin, who thought he was the bastard son of the elder Duke, finds out that he is truly the legitimate heir. James is not about to let his family home be sold off to some stranger, no matter how beautiful and sensual she is. He uses every trick he knows as a barrister to connive, seduce, and otherwise convince Bella that she needs to give back the manor to him. Bella is equally invested in keeping the home for herself where she and her companion, Harriet, can live comfortably with the rents from tenants. Things seem to be moving toward some sort of arrangement when trouble comes calling and they must work together to rid themselves of the unwanted attention, especially when it begins to turn violent. As they protect one another, Bella is forced to reconsider her feelings for James. She was not interested in anything James has to offer—except those sweet kisses they exchange have left her longing for more. Their love grows while they fight together for the land they both treasure. (Regency Barrister, #2)

Jackson, Brenda.
▶ *Courting Justice*. 2012. Kimani. ISBN 9780373534739. 299pp.

About to turn 30 and in need of a break, Attorney Peyton Mahoney takes off for two weeks in the Bahamas. Little does she know that she is being set up by her girlfriends. The resort is partially owned by longtime friend and fellow attorney D'Angelo Di Meglio, who has been infatuated with Peyton for years. He sees this trip as a way for him to finally convince her that he is the man for her. Peyton has no time in her busy life for love. Not since she was burned so badly by a former boyfriend. Her South Side Chicago roots weren't blue enough for his blue-blooded New England family. Their steamy vacation encounters have Peyton questioning her reasoning for keeping him at arm's length. D'Angelo takes his time building from their friendship to a slow-burning romance that even Peyton can't ignore. When they are on opposite sides of a huge case, the burn builds until it threatens to tear them both apart. A Madaris Family novel.

James, Julie.
Something about You. 2010. Berkley Sensation. ISBN 9780425233382. 307pp.

Several years ago, assistant U.S. attorney Cameron Lynde was the reason for a case going bad and it nearly ruined Special Agent Jack Pallas's career. Now the two are forced to work together again. Cameron is the sole witness to a high-profile murder case. Jack is assigned to investigate the case. The mystery and investigation is handled well, with the suspense running nearly as high as the sexual tension between Cameron and Jack. If they could ever stop bickering and blaming each other, they might realize how perfect of each other they are. The first in a new series by James, FBI/US Attorneys.

Shepherd, Kandy.
Love Is a Four-Legged Word. 2009. Berkley. ISBN 9780425227848. 328pp.

Poor Tom O'Brien. He is a lawyer waiting to make partner when he gets a client that might completely derail his neat and tidy life. His new client is Brutus, a mutt who is the heir to Walter Stoddard's multimillion dollar estate. There is no doubt about it, the will has left everything to Brutus and his guardian, the beautiful Maddy Cartwright. Maddy lived downstairs from Walter and adopted him as a surrogate grandfather not knowing he was uber-wealthy.

Now Tom must keep Maddy and Brutus safe and happy for the 21-day probate period. Between the media making the worst assumptions about why Maddy was named Brutus's guardian and a long-lost relative trying to wrestle her and Brutus out of the will, Maddy needs protection and a shoulder to lean on. Tom finds himself only too happy to provide both in this charming sweet romance.

Wisdom, Linda.
Wicked by Any Other Name. 2009. Sourcebooks. ISBN 9781402217739. 372pp.

The tiny town of Moonstone Lake, population 148 doesn't mind that there are witches living in their town. Stasi Romanov and her roommate Blair live there peacefully. Stasi runs a lingerie shop and sells love charms on the side. Stasi is being sued in Wizards' Court over a love spell gone wrong. Her accuser hires Trevor Barnes, wizard and superlawyer. When he comes to town to visit his client, things go from bad to worse for Stasi. As if a lawsuit wasn't enough trouble for Stasi; when she meets Trevor she sees dancing hearts over his head—the witching world sign for soul mate. Uh huh . . . witches and wizards can't be together. Everyone knows that. Cupid must be playing a joke on them. As the case progresses, so does the undeniable attraction between Trevor and Stasi. Along with the lawsuit and the dancing hearts, the townspeople seem to be turning on Stasi. Can Trevor and Stasi figure out why and fix the problem before Moonstone Lake turns into another Salem?

Romance across the Rainbow

When it comes to love, there are boys who love boys, girls who love girls, and boys and girls who love boys and girls. It is all good.

Brayden, Melissa.
Heart Block. 2012. Bold Strokes Books. ISBN 9781602827585. 264pp.

Successful business owner Emory Owen is not a woman who has many relationships. She was not particularly close to her mother and doesn't relish the task of closing out her late mother's home. The only bright spot in that task is single mom Sarah Matamoros. Sarah is helping her mother, whose cleaning team has been hired to clean and ready the home for sale. These two women could not be more different or from more diverse backgrounds, but as they spend time together readying the house, they begin to fall in love. There are obstacles to their relationship, but even obstacles can be overcome.

Herndeen, Ann.
Phyllida and the Brotherhood of Philander. 2008. Perennial. ISBN 978006 1451362. 532pp.

Andrew Carrington is a gentleman who realizes that it is time he finds a wife. Most of the women from the Ton would love to marry him. Handsome, heir to an earldom, and all around charming, he is certainly a catch. Though there is a catch, he prefers the company of men. In 1812 London, that is a highly guarded secret. He needs to find a wife who will be in agreement with his continuing membership in the Brotherhood of the Philander, a gentlemen's club for like-minded gentlemen, and to bear his sons. Phyllida, authoress of romance novels, is just the bride for him. She never thought that she would be married and agrees to his terms if Andrew agrees to allow her to continue writing. A deal is reached and the two are married. Andrew takes a male lover, Matthew Thornby. It seems as though all is working out until Phyllida is assaulted and there is a blackmail plot afoot. Not only that, but Andrew thinks he may be falling in love with his bride. A well-researched, bawdy, and delightful Regency romance.

Maxfield, Z. A.

Crossing Borders. 2008. Loose ID. ISBN 9781596327832. 316pp.

After being dumped by yet another girlfriend, Tristan is starting to think that maybe he is batting for the wrong team. He figures he can't do any worse with trying to date guys than he is by dating girls. He comes up with a crazy plan to attract his first guy. Of course, the plan goes awry, but it does bring Officer Michael Truax into his life. Officer Michael has had his eye on Tristan for several years now. They met when he gave Tristan a ticket for riding his skateboard without a helmet. Michael is more than happy to introduce Tristan to the lifestyle, but what was supposed to be a fun ride is turning into much more. Michael's concern about the difference in their ages, Tristan is 19 to his 28, almost derails their fragile relationship but not quite. Both their mothers are supportive of their sons and their choices. The sex is scorching hot, and the romance is plentiful.

Peters, Julie Ann.

Keeping You a Secret. 2005. Little Brown & Co. ISBN 9780316009850. 250pp. Ⓨ Ⓐ

High school student Holland Jaeger is drifting through life. She is going through the motions, letting others call the shots. She is content to stay busy with the student council, swim team, her boyfriend, and trying to get into a good college. Then Cece Goddard transfers to her school. Lesbian and proud, she challenges everything that Holland believes about herself and her sexuality. As their friendship turns to a flirtation and then to a serious relationship, Holland ends things with her boyfriend and suddenly finds herself the subject of discrimination and prejudice. Holland finds strength in herself that carries her through the difficulties of adjusting to a new lifestyle. A realistic and powerful look at the feelings of new love and at self-discovery.

Radclyffe.

Turn Back Time. 2006. Bold Strokes Books. ISBN 9781933110349. 208pp.

Two struggling doctors—Wynter and Pearce; they met briefly several years ago but nothing could have prepared them for the intense attraction that they would feel when meeting again. Pearce is the chief surgical resident who is trying to outrun her father's shadow. Wynter is trying to balance work life with taking care of her young child. Neither has the time or the emotional resources for a relationship. Working together is fine. Becoming friends might be okay. Anything more than that is unthinkable except that it is happening whether the women are ready for it or not. In spite of the craziness of not one but two surgeons' schedules and pressures, they manage to make this relationship work. Both romantic and sexy.

Rose, Crystal.
I'll Be Your Drill, Soldier! 2009. Dark Roast Press. ISBN 9781452482842. 186pp.

Disowned and financially cut off at 22 when he came out, Ryan needed a way to pay for college. At the time, the army seemed like the sensible choice. Ryan and his fellow soldiers are training under Drill Sergeant Phillip Grabowsky. Big, scary Sergeant Grabowsky who is featured every night in Ryan's dreams. Dreams of the nightmare and intense erotic variety. It turns out it isn't only Ryan having those dreams, not the nightmares, but the seriously sexy dreams featuring Ryan and the Sergeant. Over the course of several years, through basic training, deployments, and return trips home, Ryan and Phillip share a love that is realistic, sexy, and honest. This book is a roller coaster of laughter and sadness.

Ward, J. R.
▶ *Lover at Last*. 2013. Penguin. ISBN 9780451239358. 591pp.

Part of the long-running <u>Black Dagger Brotherhood</u> series. Vampires Qhinn and Blay have been best friends for longer than either of them can recall. They are always there for each other, whether it is fighting the war against their slayer enemies or acting as wingman for one another at a local bar. Their friendship is tested to the limits now as things are getting emotional and physical between them. Both are caught up in their own problems and need time to realize that they really are in love with one another. When they do, watch out—furniture breaks, clothes fly, and hearts open. Raw and honest, Blay and Qhinn finally get their act together and make a commitment to each other. (<u>Black Dagger Brotherhood</u>, #11)

Webb, T. A.
Second Chances. 2012. Dreamspinner. ISBN 9781623800321. 200pp.

For years, Mark Jennings has gone to Antonio Roberto for a massage. Mark is breaking up with his boyfriend Brian, Mark's mother is dying . . . his life is a mess, but Antonio is a constant in it. Over the years, they become closer than either of them either expected. When Brian comes back into Mark's life, Antonio is there to listen and to be there when tragedy strikes. The change in Mark and Antonio's relationship from friends to lovers is subtle but it progresses from such a deep friendship that it seems completely natural. There is a side plot dealing with Antonio's son Jason and one of the boys at the shelter where Mark works that is well done. A true tearjerker before Antonio and Mark get their happily ever after.

Who Wrote the Book of Love?

They're something so romantic about the written word. Readers will enjoy these books about authors and bookstores.

Dahl, Victoria.
Talk Me Down. 2009. HQN Books. ISBN 9780373773565. 347pp.

When her ex-boyfriend begins stalking her, Molly Jennings decides it is time to leave Denver and head home to tiny Tumble Creek, Colorado. Molly hopes to run into her first crush and the inspiration for her erotic novels, Ben Lawson. No one, including her family, knows what she does for a living and she intends to keep it that way. When Molly meets up with Ben again, the attraction is instant, but while she's just hoping for a little fun, Ben wants something more. Ben, now the chief of police, senses that Molly is hiding something, but after a scandal tore his family apart when he was still in high school, he doesn't do secrets. When Molly's past comes back to haunt her, will Ben be there to protect her? Dahl started with historical romances; this is her debut contemporary romance and in the last few years, she's gone back and forth between contemporary and historical. This is seriously steamy—the heroine enjoys dirty talk in bed; but there is also a lot of laughs. Molly is sassy and tough; Ben is hot and sensitive.

Hart, Regina.
Trinity Falls. 2013. Dafina. ISBN 9780758286529. 384pp.

Six months after his father's death, Ean Fever decides he needs to change his life. He resigns from his partnership with a prestigious New York City law firm and returns home to tiny Trinity Falls, Ohio. He discovers that many things are not like he remembered them, especially Megan McCloud—she's grown from a shy awkward girl into a stunningly beautiful woman. Bakery owner Megan McCloud has had a crush on Ean for years, but her competitive older cousin Ramona has a history of going after whatever Megan wants. Years ago, Ramona followed Ean to New York; now, as mayor of Trinity Falls, she is going after Megan's bakery, but Megan has learned to fight for what she wants and she's not giving up so easily this time. (Finding Home, #1)

Kaye, Robin.
Call Me Wild. 2012. Sourcebooks Casablanca. ISBN 9781402257339. 352pp.

When sports writer Jessie James is laid off, she moves to Boise, Idaho, to write a romance novel. Jessie doesn't believe in love and has never read a romance, but everyone knows how easy it is to write a romance. Arriving in Boise, Jessie runs into Fisher Kincaid repeatedly. Could she have attracted a stalker already? Fisher, who may just be the perfect man, falls for Jessie, but it takes her longer to warm up to him. When his sister Karma plots to get them alone together in the family's lakeside cabin, he offers to teach Jessie everything she needs to know to write her novel. Can Jessie learn about love without falling in love? This is the second book in the <u>Wild Thing</u> series, the first is about Fisher's twin, Hunter. Secondary characters play a big part and presumably Kaye plans to give each of the other siblings their own books in the future. Unique characters and situations, humor, and just enough sex combine for a fast-paced enjoyable read.

Klassen, Julie.
The Girl in the Gatehouse. 2010. Bethany House. ISBN 9780764207082. 391pp.

Banished by her father after a scandal, Mariah Aubrey lives in the abandoned gatehouse on the edge of a distant aunt's estate with only her former nanny as a companion. Mariah supports herself by writing novels under a pseudonym. She meets Captain Matthew Bryant when he rents the estate, hoping to show Isabella, a woman who rejected him years ago for being poor and not of the same social standing, what a mistake she has made. Captain Bryant is fascinated by Mariah but determined to marry Isabella. As he learns more about Mariah, he's not sure he wants to be connected to someone who behaved so scandalously. Mariah's story is slowly revealed, and readers don't learn all the details of the scandal until the final third of the book. Mariah struggles with her past but is finally able to forgive herself and find forgiveness from God. Taking inspiration from Jane Austen, Klassen includes detailed descriptions of life during the early 1800s. Secondary characters are well realized, quirky, and not always what they appear to be.

Kramer, Kieran.
▶ *Cloudy with a Chance of Marriage*. 2011. St. Martin's. ISBN 9780312374037. 416pp.

After years in an abusive arranged marriage, Jilly Jones runs away to London with Otis, her trusty retainer. She buys Hodgepodge, a bookstore on the aptly named Dreare Street, where the sun never shines. Captain Stephen Arrow, one of the Regent's impossible Bachelors, is living it up down the street in a house that he inherited and is trying to sell. When Stephen's obnoxious relatives show up with an unmarried daughter that they'd like him to marry, he makes a deal with Jilly. She agrees to pretend that they are courting in exchange for a favor. A comical cast of well-developed secondary characters provides an entertaining backdrop for this battle of wits, which sparks into romance. (<u>Impossible Bachelors</u>, #3)

Ridgway, Christie.
Beach House No. 9. 2013. HQN Books. ISBN 9780373777402. 384pp.

Jane Pearson is a book doctor—she helps authors struggling with their manuscripts turn in a finished product. After spending years with bestselling author Ian Stone, and being publicly acknowledged as his muse, she suddenly found her reputation being tarnished by him when she ends their professional relationship after he cheats on her in their personal relationship. Jane is then hired by Griffin Lowell's agent to get his memoir about his years as a war journalist in order. Griffin was witness to a lot of horrible events in Afghanistan and is suffering from posttraumatic stress disorder. He uses alcohol and partying as a way to shut everyone out. Jane is determined to get his attention and get him to focus on writing the book. At first, she only wants to get the book written to undo the damage to her career, but as time passes, she falls for him. The hero and heroine are fully developed characters who are both suffering and vulnerable. A secondary plotline about Griffin's sister Tess's marriage is a great contrast to Jane and Griffin's developing relationship. Jane also has the best wardrobe of sexy shoes and even sexier underwear of any romance character ever.

Stacey, Shannon.
  Exclusively Yours. 2011. HQN Books. ISBN 9780373776788. 352pp.
      Keri Daniels and Joe Kowalski had the type of high school romance that everyone dreams of, but Keri broke it off right after graduation to pursue a career. Almost 20 years have passed and Keri is a journalist for an entertainment magazine in Los Angeles, while Joe is a reclusive bestselling horror writer, still living in New Hampshire. When her boss discovers that Keri and Joe dated once upon a time, she is given an ultimatum—get the story or get a new job. Joe agrees to answer Keri's questions, but she must accompany him on the family camping trip and she can only ask one question for each day that she stays. The sparks between them are still there and being in close quarters is making that hard to ignore, but Keri loves her life in Los Angeles and Joe wants to stay in New Hampshire. The Kowalski family is delightful; the characters are real people who are struggling with all of the different issues found in the modern world. The secondary plotline about Keri's ex-BFF/Joe's twin sister Terry and her marital problems adds depth to the story. Heartbreak, happiness, humor—you'll find it all here. (Kowalski Family, #1)

Librarians in Love

Librarians don't always do it by the books.

Austin, Lynn.
  Wonderland Creek. 2011. Bethany House. ISBN 9780764204985. 400pp.
      Librarian Alice Grace Ripley lives most of her life vicariously, through the pages of whatever book she happens to be reading at the moment. After her boyfriend catches her reading during a patron's funeral, he breaks up with her; shortly after that, she loses her job due to the economy. Alice decides to leave Chicago with the boxes of donated books she has collected and heads

for the mountains of eastern Kentucky during the Great Depression. Arriving in the tiny coal mining town of Acorn, Alice is forced to grow up and face reality. She meets head librarian Leslie "Mack" MacDougal and becomes a pack horse librarian, delivering books to the isolated and destitute families in the mountains. Mack and Alice share a love of books, and the bonds between them grow after he is shot and Alice takes care of him. The romance is sweet and understated. Austin is wonderfully descriptive in her writing; she brings to life an era long gone. The pack horse librarians are based on Roosevelt's Work Projects Administration program, which hired women to deliver books and magazines to remote areas of Kentucky.

Bardsley, Michelle.
Don't Talk Back to Your Vampire. 2007. Signet Eclipse. ISBN 9780451221704. 340pp.
　　The paranormal is perfectly normal in Broken Heart, Oklahoma. The town is a mix of vampire, werewolves, and a few humans. When vampire elder Lorcan became sick with the taint, he attacked nearly a dozen people at a PTA meeting, including single mom and local librarian Eva LaRue. They were all turned into vampires. Lorcan and Eva seem to have a lot in common, especially their love of books, but can you really fall in love with the vampire who killed you? Quirky characters, a fast-paced plot, and lots of humor make the second book in the <u>Broken Heart Oklahoma</u> series a quick, fun read.

Havens, Candace.
Like a Charm. 2008. Berkley Trade. ISBN 978042519263. 289pp.
　　Lawyer Kira Smythe never intended to return home to Sweet, Texas. Sweet was protected by a coven of witches and most of the residents had some kind of magical powers. Kira never did and always felt a little out of place. Then a coworker commits suicide in front of her, and Kira gets mono. She goes home to Sweet to recuperate before returning to her high-powered job. While she's there, the local librarian dies and leaves the library to Kira, as long as she stays and becomes the new librarian. A sexy visiting reporter named Caleb who makes her tingle, her new found ability to talk to the dead, and the threatening notes that she is receiving give Kira plenty to think about. Kira is an incredibly likeable character, the secondary characters are interesting (especially the ghosts), and the romance is sweet with just a little spice.

Linz, Cathie.
Luck Be a Lady. 2010. Berkeley. ISBN 9780425237830. 292pp.
　　Librarian Megan West is determined that nothing will go wrong during her best friend/cousin Faith's wedding in Las Vegas. Chicago cop Logan Doyle rushes in before the "I dos" and demands that the wedding be stopped because the groom is still married. Fortunately, it turns out to be a misunderstanding, but it does mean that Megan and Logan don't exactly hit it off. After

discovering that her mother, whom she's been told died when she was two, is still alive, she runs into Logan again. He's always been a sucker for a damsel in distress, and there does seem to be some chemistry between them, so he offers to help Megan find her mother. Linz seems to have a special place in her heart for librarians; several of her heroines share the occupation, and there is nothing stereotypical about them. The secondary characters are quirky, the pacing is fast, and the sexual tension sizzles. (West Investigations, #2)

Love, Kathy.
Wanting What You Get. 2004. Zebra. ISBN 9780821776131. 352pp.
    The second book in the Stepp Sisters trilogy is middle sister Ellie's story. Librarian Ellie Stepp has always been shy and a little overweight. At her sister's wedding reception, Mason Sweet, the guy she's been crushing on for most of her life, flirts with her. Mason, a former high school football player and all-around golden boy, has become the mayor of their little town. When budget cuts threaten the library, Ellie goes to Mason, and he offers to help her out if she'll sleep with him. Seeing this as a way to live out her fantasies, Ellie accepts his offer and they begin an affair. Both Ellie and Mason have issues; Ellie has a hard time accepting that anyone can find her attractive due to her low self-esteem and Mason is an alcoholic. Love's characters are real people with real problems. Addiction plot lines aren't usually found in romance novels, but the author portrays Mason's struggles realistically.

Mallery, Susan.
▶ *Summer Nights*. 2012. HQN Books. ISBN 9780373776870. 384pp.
    After getting out of a bad marriage and returning to Fool's Gold, California, Shane Stryker has decided to marry a nice, quiet uncomplicated woman. When he sees a gorgeous redhead dancing on the bar, he knows she is trouble and makes a beeline for the nearest exit. He agrees to let his mother fix him up with the perfect woman, Annabelle Weiss, a librarian who wants to learn to ride a horse. When Annabelle turns out to be the dancer from the bar and not the mousy wallflower he was expecting, Shane is drawn to her but unwilling to believe that she's not like his ex-wife. Annabelle is attracted to him, too, but after a disastrous first marriage, she's not willing to settle. This is the eighth entry in Mallery's Fool's Gold series and many characters from previous books are featured prominently. Strong family ties, a sense of community, and some spicy love scenes make this an enjoyable addition to the series.

McGary, Lucinda.
The Treasures of Venice. 2009. Sourcebooks. ISBN 9781402226700. 334pp.
    After her fiancé dumps her three weeks before their wedding, librarian Samantha Lewis decides to take their nonrefundable honeymoon trip to Italy by herself. While sitting at a café in Venice, she is approached by a hot

Irish stranger who pretends to know her and she decides to play along. When Kiernan Fitzgerald shows up in her hotel room later that night bleeding, Sam is drawn into his search. Kiernan's historian sister was kidnapped and the ransom is the legendary Jewels of the Madonna. The present-day story alternates with flashbacks to 1485, when Serafina Lombardo, the daughter of a wealthy family, is to marry her deceased sister's husband. Instead, she falls in love with sculptor Nino Andriotto. Laced with passion and suspense, McGary draws you in as the tension mounts and the story behind the jewels' disappearance unfolds.

Morsi, Pamela.
Love Overdue. 2013. MIRA. ISBN 9780778315377. 432pp.

Arriving in the small town of Verdant, Kansas, Dorothy "DJ" Jarrow is excited to be taking over as the library director. DJ fits the librarian stereotype to a T; she's quiet and conservative and has several pairs of sensible shoes and a dog named Melville Dewey Jr. She's been offered a room in the home of the library board president, Viv Sanderson, but doesn't realize at first that Viv is more interested in having her accept another position—wife of her pharmacist son, Scott. When DJ meets Scott, she's shocked to discover that he was her Spring Break fling eight years ago when she decided to see if she had a wild side. She's ready to pack up and move when she realizes that Scott doesn't remember her. At first she is relieved, but she soon finds herself hoping for a second chance with Scott. Fans of quirky characters, small-town settings with all the usual gossip, and witty dialogues will find themselves hoping for their own book of love.

Multicultural Heroes and Heroines

A selection of romances features non-Caucasian heroes/heroines.

African American

Allers, Rochelle.
Sanctuary Cove. 2011. Forever. ISBN 9781455501403. 338pp.

After her husband died amid a scandal, Deborah Robinson moves her two teen children and herself back home to the small lowland town where her grandparents lived, Cavanagh Island, South Carolina. Here she opens a bookstore and tries to begin again. Dr. Asa Monroe is a snowbird spending the winter when he begins working at the bookstore. The attraction between Asa and Deborah is immediate but they are both still grieving. Asa lost his wife and child not long ago. Since then he has been wandering trying to find a reason to stay put. Working at the bookstore together, they tentatively begin to act upon their attraction. If they can navigate around the obstacles they encounter, they may get a second chance at love. The beginning of the <u>Cavanagh Island</u> series this entry introduces readers to the slightly eccentric residents of the town that oozes southern small-town charm.

Hodges, Cheris.
Forces of Nature. 2013. Kensington/Dafina. ISBN 9780758276605. 384pp.

Farming the land that her family has owned for generations is what Crystal Hughes lives for. She's proud to be part of the first African American family that owned a farm in Duval, North Carolina, and of what it has become. Douglas Wellington III is heir to Welco Industries. Welco has had their eyes on the Hughes's farm and now is the time to buy it. Not going down without a fight, Crystal convinces Douglas to spend a week on the farm in hopes that he will see how wrong it is to destroy it. Douglas agrees only because he is completely smitten by Crystal. Spending a week together ignites a passion between them that is impossible to ignore.

Jenkins, Beverly.
▶ *Destiny's Embrace*. 2013. Avon. ISBN 9780062032652. 384pp.

In 1885, Mariah Cooper is offered the chance to escape her dreary life in Philadelphia by answering an advertisement for a housekeeper in California. She has no idea just how much her life is going to change now that she is out from under her mother's cruel hand. Her new employer is handsome, wealthy, and stubborn as a mule, Logan. Logan's stepmother hired Mariah without consulting Logan and he isn't sure he needs an uppity Easterner keeping house for him. Locking horns with him brings out a feistiness Mariah never knew she had. If only they can stop bickering long enough to see the attraction that lies beneath the surface. A visit from Mariah's past catapults her and Logan into each other's arms.

Asian

Dimon, HelenKay.
Impulsive. 2010. Brava. ISBN 9780758229090. 268pp.

Being in Oahu, Hawaii, should have been like being in paradise. But for Japanese American Eric Kumura, it is not quite so. He's in town to attend the wedding of his former girlfriend and to show voters (he is running for office) that he is a stand-up guy. At the wedding he indulges in a little anonymous hookup with one of the waitresses working the event. Feeling badly about the way he treated her, Eric goes looking for the waitress. He finds Katie Long, 25 years old and trying to right her wrongs by working for her sister's catering company. Sparks fly and they once again hit the sheets. What he thinks is a casual flirtation is twofold. Katie is actually working to get information on him for the opposing candidate, but she is beginning to have real feelings for Eric. He needs to know that even though she is totally wrong for him, she won't ruin his chances with the voters. If he finds out who she is working for and why, will he still want to see her? Fans of romantic suspense will enjoy it for the political intrigue.

McCarty, Sarah.
Shadow's Stand. 2012. HQN Books. ISBN 9780373777051. 377pp.

Moments before Shadow Ochoa is about to be hung for horse thieving, Fei Yen invokes a little known law and claims him as her husband. In Western Kansas, 1859, a woman cannot hold property and she needs a man's name to claim the land she is prospecting. He is a name to put on a piece of paper; that is all. Shadow doesn't like the way that Fei bosses him around but figures he will deal with it since he enjoys their steamy nights together. Trouble is just around the corner for these newlyweds as bounty hunters are on Shadow's trail and Fei has enemies that would see her dead as well. They will need to learn to trust one another if they are to survive. A solid entry into the Hell's Eight series.

Interracial

Matthews, Lena.
Happily Even After. 2010. Loose ID. ISBN 9781607377436. 228pp.

Creigh and Dean have been divorced for almost a year. Theirs was not a divorce born out of major issues . . . they simply thought that the marriage ran its course. For the sake of their two children, they keep up a façade of cheerfulness. Truth be told they are both miserable and completely still in love with each other. Then Creigh finds out she is pregnant by a one-night stand. Not knowing what she is going to do or how she is going to do it, Dean steps in and takes over. He helps Creigh through the pregnancy and together they rediscover and admit their feelings. Theirs is a very real relationship; they argue, they fight, and they make up. In the end, Dean makes it clear that it doesn't matter that he is not the biological father, this child will be "his." How can you not fall in love with such a devoted family man? Warning—seriously hot bedroom scenes with very dirty talk.

Smith, Maureen.
Romancing the M.D. 2011. Kimani. ISBN 9780373862290. 218pp.

Love and hate are two sides of the same coin. At least that is the way it is for Dr. Tamara St. John, intern at Hopewell General and Dr. Victor Aguilar. The two clash over everything to the point where even the staff is getting concerned. After a particularly grueling night in the hospital, they spend the early morning hours talking and find that although they are as different as can be, he is Colombian, she is African American, they have a tremendous amount in common. If they can stop bickering long enough to see it, they would make a great couple. Besides the bickering, not only do hospital rules forbid a relationship, Victor's family is against a relationship for him with anyone except a Colombian woman. Will these two make it against all the odds stacked up against them? Neither one is a wallflower, and they are determined to make it work. Part of the Hopewell General series.

Riding on the Edge

Books about bikers, their old ladies, and more.

Ashley, Kristen.
Own the Wind. 2013. Forver. ISBN 9781455599257. 389pp.

    Taking place over the course of several years, Tabby and Shy's story is not an easy one. Tabby has grown up in the Chaos Motorcycle Club. Her dad, Tack, is the Head of the Club. She's been around bikers, bitches, and old ladies since she was a baby. Now she's all grown up and has her heart set on Parker "Shy" Cage. She's had a mad crush on him for a very long time. She knows that she is off limits to the club, so she seeks love outside the club. When her fiancé is killed in a car crash, she turns to Shy to help her get over it and to get her head on straight. After months of being together as friends, they take the leap to lovers; they heat things up in a big way! Tabby and Shy may bicker about housekeeping and where they are going to live, but the sex is always hot and heavy. They are in for more problems when the club finds out about their relationship and Tabby's best friend gets the club involved in a fight they might not be able to win. Through it all, Tabby and Shy weather the storms and come out stronger for it. This is the first book in the <u>Chaos</u> series.

Jamieson, Kelly.
Hot Ride. 2013. Samhain. ISBN 9781619213586. 270pp.

    Sera Manning has shut her heart off. Everyone who she was close to died, abandoned, or betrayed her. Now working as a Drug Enforcement Administration agent, she is about to go undercover to bring down the organization that she blames for destroying her life. Her soon-to-be partner, Ryan Thomas, needs a girlfriend to authenticate his place with the bikers. Ryan's not thrilled with having a newbie on his team, but he has no choice. The chemistry between Sera and Ryan ensures that their pretending to be a couple is smoking hot. It is never a good idea to get involved romantically or sexually with your partner, but these two can't deny what is happening. This novel realistically portrays undercover agents who are struggling to keep their roles straight. Sera for the first time has girlfriends as she hangs out and gets to know the old ladies of the club. Ryan is starting to like the bikers more and more. Separating their undercover personas from real life is getting harder and harder. Keeping their love a secret is becoming impossible.

Kauffman, Donna.
Here Comes Trouble. 2010. Brava. ISBN 9780758231338. 200pp.

    Kirby Farrell is beginning a new chapter in her life. She has left a bad relationship, opened up a bed and breakfast in Vermont, and is hoping that global warming really is a fluke. Brett Hennessey is heading out of Vegas on the back of his bike looking to outrun trouble. He doesn't expect to find trouble in Vermont but what he does find is a pretty lady who pushes all his buttons. Kirby isn't sure what to make of this sexy biker boy more years than she cares to admit her junior. She is afraid that she isn't right for him or young enough while Brett has his hands full when he finds out that what happens in Vegas doesn't always stay in Vegas. A sizzling sexy read.

Linz, Cathie.
Good Girls Do. 2006. Berkley. ISBN 9780425208489. 336pp.

Serenity Falls, Pennsylvania, is the idyllic home of Julia Wright. She made it her home after years of living a hippie lifestyle with her mother and sister. Now she works at the local Library, has a home, and is quite happy. Until two things happen. Angela, her hippie mother, arrives to stay with her along with her thief of a sister, her four-year-old niece and their two llamas. At the same time, local boy gone bad, Luke Maguire rides into town on the back of his Harley. Luke is only in town long enough to meet the terms set in his father's will. He needs to work at the family bar for six months and then he can sell it if he wants. What he really wants is to steal some more kisses from the increasingly frazzled Julia. It is time she let go of her good side and give in to the Harley riding side. Funny and sexy, this is a lighter take on the Biker Romance.

Shalvis, Jill.
Her Sexiest Mistake. 2005. Signet. ISBN 9780451217097. 314pp.

Leaving behind her trailer park roots, Mia Appleby has made a good life for herself. She has a great job and a home of her own. She has left all the remnants of her past except for the one where she refuses to commit to a man. Mia is a love 'em and leave 'em kind of gal. The queen of one-night stands. Until she gets a sexy new bike-riding neighbor. Being the neighborly type, she brings him cookies and a night of mind-blowing sex as way of the welcome wagon. It turns out that her new neighbor, high school teacher Kevin, is looking for more than a one-night stand. While Mia repeatedly comes calling for some booty, Kevin is trying to get her to commit. Add in a visit from Mia's past and Kevin's younger brother, and you have the makings of a fun, sexy, and engaging read.

Walker, Julie Ann.
Hell on Wheels. 2012. Sourcebooks. ISBN 9781402267130. 364pp.

Ali Morgan has always had her eye on ex-Marine Nate Weller, but he still sees her as his best friend, Grigg's baby sister. When Grigg is killed, Ali gets into a heap of trouble with a sinister organization that now has her in their target. The custom bike shop where Nate works is really a cover for a special operations unit that is out to find out what happened to Grigg and to keep Ali safe. Ali's more than okay with that, Nate is sex on wheels on his bike, and Ali intends to enjoy every moment of the ride! Fast paced, high sexual tension, and steamy love scenes add up to one hot ride in this series opener.

Wylde, Joana.

▶ *Reaper's Property*. 2013. Ellora's Cave. ISBN 9781419970290. 306pp.

Marie is trying to pick up the pieces after leaving an abusive marriage. She is staying with her brother and that's when the trouble starts. Horse, a huge tattooed biker, starts hanging around her brother's place to do some business with her brother. Horse usually gets whatever he wants, and he wants Marie. He wants her badly, but she isn't ready for a relationship. Things go from bad to worse when her brother steals from Horse's motorcycle club, the Reapers. The Reapers need to be paid but with no money, Marie is offered as collateral if she gives it up for Horse. He comes to care for her and wants her to be his old lady. Marie slowly comes to terms with the biker lifestyle. She has feelings for Horse, more than she wants to admit. Horse can be rough with Marie, which may put off some readers, but he is a bit of a teddy bear with her too. There is some very hot sex, almost public sex, and crazy ass biker sex.

Chapter Three

Mood

Romance readers are in the mood for love, but there's something more they're looking for as well. Readers are invested emotionally in these books, and consequently, they're happy when the characters are and sad when they are, too.

Mood is the overarching feeling of a novel. It can be scary, sad, suspenseful, or steamy. It is the atmosphere of the book. Readers may choose to read a book that matches their mood or one that is completely contrary to their mood. They may choose a steamy one to spice things up for them. Reading is an active experience, and readers' moods affect the way they see a book. These lists each evoke a certain feeling. Use them when a reader asks for something spooky or something to make them cry.

Fangs for the Memories

Fangs take the mundane everyday world and add a supernatural undertone to it. A perfect foil for the heated romances found in their pages.

Ann, Brooklyn.
Bite Me, Your Grace. 2013. Sourcebooks. ISBN 9781402274442. 352pp.
Angelica Winthrop is bound and determined to become the next literary sensation in London. She is convinced that she can be just as successful as Mary Shelley, whose fascinating book has sent the Ton into a frenzy. Her mother wants her to marry and be a wife and mother. Marriage would ruin her writing career, so Angelica decides to ruin her reputation so no man will have her. Her neighbor, Ian Ashton, the Duke of Burnrath, is living a double life. He is a

respected member of the Ton but also the Vampire Lord of London! While doing a little breaking and entering to research the mysterious Lord Ian, Angelica accidentally discovers his dark secret. Knowing that the Ton will have a field day with her and her sullied reputation now that she has been alone with a man, Ian offers to marry Angelica to protect her. What's a girl to do? Reluctantly she agrees to marry the handsome lord. It is not love at first sight for these two newlyweds. Misunderstandings abound, but when the two of these work those out, the sparks begin to fly. A fun and witty take on both the Regency romance and the vampire romance. First in the <u>Bite Me, Your Grace</u> series.

Cole, Kresley. ♛
A Hunger like No Other. 2006. Pocket Star. ISBN 9781416509875. 360pp.

Laclain MacRieve, clan leader of the Lykae werewolves, has been tortured for centuries by the local vampire horde. He loathes vampires as a result. The only thing keeping him somewhat sane during his torture is the thought of his soul mate. He knows she is out there; he can sense her. When he finds her, she is the young, sheltered Emmaline. When he finds her, he coerces her back to his ancestral home in Scotland, unaware that she is half Valkyrie and half vampire. She is shocked to discover that he is a Lykae, who are known for being brutes and horrible to their mates. He is horrified to discover she is half vampire. They must put aside their prejudices as they begin a courtship dance that soothes the beast in both of them. Together they must face down their enemies and learn to build a life that works for his Lykae side and her vampire side—not an easy task. (<u>Immortals after Dark</u>, #2)

Harper, Molly.
▶ *The Care and Feeding of Stray Vampires*. 2012. Pocket Books. ISBN 978 1451641837. 356pp.

Iris Scanlon of Half-Moon Hollow runs her business, Beeline, while taking care of her younger sister. The business is odd, but it pays the bills. She runs daytime errands for the town's vampire population. When she gets to a meeting with her newest client, Cletus "Cal" Calix, he is on the floor poisoned. Naturally he persuades Iris to hide him in her home until he can recover and find out who wants him dead for good. Going against all her rules and reservations, she allows it, for a price. While he is recuperating, Iris's knowledge of plants and botany help with his investigation. Filled with Harper's trademark snarky dialogue and flat-out sexy heroes, this first entry into the <u>Half Moon Hollow</u> series is a light-and-fun read. It doesn't hurt that in between bickering and trying to solve the mystery of the poison, they are getting busy with each other.

Humphreys, Sara.
Tall Dark and Vampire. 2013. Sourcebooks Casablanca. ISBN 9781402274060. 312pp.

When vampires dream, it usually means trouble since they don't as a rule dream. Nightclub owner and vampire Olivia Hollingsworth is shaken when she begins to dream for the first time in more years than she can count. Her dreams are of Doug Paxton, the man she loved but who died centuries ago. Fortunately for Olivia, she has more to deal with than her strange dreams. Vampires are being murdered, and they are being linked to her club. The cop investigating the murders turns out to be Doug reincarnated. He too has been having disturbing dreams. He cannot believe that the woman from his dreams is real, but Olivia is flesh and blood and determined not to let him get away again. While investigating the murders, they get reacquainted in and out of bed. This is the first book in the <u>Dead in the City</u> series, a spinoff series based on Sara's popular <u>Amoveo</u> series.

Kenyon, Sherrilyn.
Night Embrace. 2003. St. Martin's. ISBN 9780312984823. 408pp.

The third entry into Kenyon's popular <u>Dark Hunter</u> series set in New Orleans. This one focuses on vampire Talon of Morrigantes, who is a Dark Hunter sworn by the goddess Artemis to protect innocents from a rogue sect of vampires. Before his death 1,500 years ago, he was betrayed by those he loved. Now he is cursed, and any woman he loves will die. To prevent that from happening, he has shut that part of himself down. No attachments, no emotions, no mess. Until he meets artist Sunshine Runningwolf. She isn't looking for commitment, having already been divorced but something about Talon won't let her treat this like another fling. Nor will it let Talon treat Sunshine that way. Their attraction is instant, intense, and hot. These two are hell-bent on not falling in love, but they fail miserably at that. This can be read as a stand-alone text, but readers will understand Kenyon's world better if they read the books in order.

Sands, Lynsay.
A Quick Bite. 2005. Avon. ISBN 9780060773755. 374pp.

If you are a vampire, it is probably not a good thing for you to faint at the sight of blood. Sadly, Lissiana Argeneau is such a creature. Her mother gives her a birthday present that she hopes will cheer her up and cure this problem. Her gift is Greg Hewitt, a psychologist who specializes in treating phobias. From the moment Lissiana lays eyes on the very yummy-looking Greg, she is head over heels in love and dying to sink her fangs into that neck of his. Greg puts the pieces together and figures out that his captors are vampires. Once he accepts that, he begins to accept Lissiana's advances. After all, how bad can a quick nibble on the neck be? Part of the <u>Argeneau</u> series. Perfect for a light, humorous look at vampire romances.

Showalter, Gena.
The Darkest Night. 2010. Harlequin. ISBN 9780373775224. 379pp.

Pandora's box was opened long ago by 12 immortal warriors. Together they unleashed the very worst the world had to offer. In return, now the warriors are cursed with whichever evil they stole. For Maddox, it is violence.

Each night he dies a violent death and is taken to hell only to be brought back the next morning. It is a horrid existence, but he manages to survive with the help of his warrior brothers. Together they live in a secluded mansion on the hill. Ashlyn is searching for these men. She has to find the source for the voices in her head that torment her. Finding her wandering their compound, Maddox kidnaps Ashlyn to protect her. Oddly the voices in her head calm when he is near. While being held captive, sparks fly and danger abounds. Ashlyn is determined to end Maddox's curse so they can be together freely. Liberally borrowed from Greek mythology, hot alpha males and steamy sex scenes make this a great beginning to the Lords of the Underworld series.

Ghosts

Finding true love can be just as scary as encountering the supernatural.

Cole, Kresley.
Dark Needs at Night's Edge. 2007. Mira. ISBN 9780778324300. 379pp.

Conrad was a member of a secret vampire hunting organization, until his brothers forced him to become one of them. Driven nearly mad by bloodlust, Conrad is taken by his brothers to a rundown estate to prevent him from harming anyone. He is chained to a bed and watched over by his brothers while they wait to see if a magical elixir will restore him or if they will have to destroy him. There he encounters Neomi Laress, a former burlesque dancer who became a prima ballerina. Murdered by her ex-fiancé in 1927, and trapped at Elancourt ever since, no one has been able to see her until now. Conrad believes his fractured mind has conjured her, but gradually they develop a relationship. Can a ghost and a vampire find love and happiness? Cole excels at world-building, and the fifth book of the Immortals after Dark series is a fast-paced read.

Crusie, Jennifer.
Maybe This Time. 2010. St. Martin's Press. ISBN 9780312303785. 342pp.

Crusie takes on Henry James's classic *The Turn of the Screw* and makes it her own in this paranormal romance. Andromeda "Andie" Miller is engaged to be married and wants to make a clean break from her ex-husband North. She goes to his office intending to return 10 years' worth of uncashed alimony check, and leaves having agreed to be a nanny. A distant cousin of North's has recently died, and he has become the guardian for two kids, who have already run off three other nannies in a haunted house. With more humor than horror, the characters are both realistic and relatable. Andie is a strong character who confronts difficult situations head on, and it soon becomes apparent that North and Andie still have a lot to work out. The chemistry is still there, but relationships aren't easy when opposites attract.

Kleypas, Lisa.
Dream Lake. 2012. St. Martin's Griffin. ISBN 9781250008299. 384pp.

 Abandoned by her mother at a young age, Zoe Hoffman was raised by her grandmother. Now her grandmother has dementia, and Zoe is taking care of her. Needing to renovate the cottage, Zoe hires Alex Nolan. Alex's ex-wife left him with almost nothing, and the downturn in the economy is taking care of the rest. Alex copes by drinking himself into oblivion. The youngest of three brothers, he spent the most time with his neglectful, alcoholic parents. Alex has also attracted a ghost, who seems to be connected to Zoe's grandmother. The Friday Harbor series has light paranormal elements, and the third book begins from the ghost's point of view. Well-developed characters, magic, and romance are key elements in this story, which is both heartbreaking and hopeful. (Friday Harbor, #3)

McCarthy, Erin.
Seeing Is Believing. 2013. Berkley. ISBN 9780425261736. 271pp.

 When Piper Tucker was eight years old, her stepfather left her with her father, who hadn't known before that moment that she existed. Piper has always wanted to be normal, but her ability to see ghosts makes her feel different. The last person she told was Brady, her babysitter and childhood crush. After a dozen years away, Brady is back from Chicago, unemployed, broke, and with no ideas for what he wants to do next. He shows up at the house where Piper is babysitting and before long they wind up in bed together. Piper knows that Brady will break her heart when he leaves, but she can't ignore the chemistry between them. A sweet and sexy romance with a light ghost mystery. (Cuttersville, #3)

Miles, Cindy.
Spirited Away. 2007. Signet Eclipse. ISBN 9780451221452. 336pp.

 A curse was placed on Tristan de Barre when he and his men were murdered in 1292. More than 700 years later, forensic anthropologist Dr. Andrea Monroe is hired to excavate old bones that were recently unearthed after a storm at Dreadmoor Castle. This isn't the first time that Andi has visited Dreadmoor. As a teenager, she was fascinated by the legend of Dragonhawk, a knight who disappeared without a trace, and while exploring, almost fell to her death before being rescued by a knight clad in chainmail. As Andi unravels the mysteries surrounding Tristan and his men, she becomes determined to break the curse, but what kind of relationship can you have when you fall in love with a ghost? An interesting combination of the modern and the medieval, this ghost story has something for everyone.

Roberts, Nora.
▶ *The Next Always*. 2011. Berkley Trade. ISBN 9780425243213. 352pp.

 When her husband is killed during his second tour in Iraq, Claire Brewster is left a widow with two young sons and a third on the way. She returns to her hometown of Boonsboro, Maryland, to run Turn the Page, the local bookstore. She can't help bumping into Beckett Montgomery, who with his brothers, Ryder and Owen, is restoring the town's historic old inn. Beckett was in love with Claire all through high school and was brokenhearted when she married his best friend Clint. The relationship that develops between Beckett and Claire is realistic; Claire is a single mom and has her share of child care issues. Family and friendship are at the core of this romance, which includes lots of girls' nights. A ghost, details about the inn's restoration, and a stalker fill out the rest of the first book in the trilogy, which continues with *The Last Boyfriend*.

Terry, Candis.
Second Chance at the Sugar Shack. 2011. Avon Impulse. ISBN 9780062115720. 336pp.

Ten years ago, Kate Silver left town after a fight with her mother about following her dream; now, Kate is the Hollywood stylist of choice to the stars. Forced to return home to Deer Lick, Montana, for her mother's funeral, Kate intends to return to her glamorous life in a day or two, but neither her brother nor her sister is able to stay behind to help her father at the family bakery. Kate's trip home is extended as she reconnects with her high school sweetheart, who is now a hunky cop and reconciles with her mother, who refused to go into the light and offers advice from the backseat of her ancient Buick. Readers who love stories set in small towns will love this sizzling romance with quirky characters, and just a touch of the paranormal. (Sugar Shack trilogy, #1)

In Sickness and in Health

When taking wedding vows, "in sickness and in health" is included. Most couples don't face the types of medical issues these couples do. Sometimes it tears them apart; sometimes it brings them closer.

Garvis-Graves, Tracey.
▶ *On the Island*. 2012. Penguin. ISBN 9781405910217. 347pp.

Almost-17-year-old T. J. Callahan is recovering from cancer and is looking forward to spending the summer catching up with friends. His family has other ideas, a vacation in the Maldives to celebrate along with a tutor to catch him up with his schoolwork. His tutor is 30-year-old Anna Emerson, who is eager to escape her quickly going downhill relationship and spend some time on the beach. They never make it to the Maldives. Their plane crashes into the Indian Ocean, when their pilot suffers a fatal heart attack. Anna and T.J. make it to an uninhabited island, where they will spend the next several years. Together they face the massive challenges ahead of them, including survival, shelter, food, and fighting disease. T.J. and Anna become more than friends, more than tutor and student and only after T.J. is over

18, lovers. Their biggest challenge of all is what happens when they are rescued and forced back into society. A beautiful story of love in the face of too
many obstacles. Readers looking for more about T.J. and Anna can download
the novella, *Uncharted.*

Goodman, Jo.
Marry Me. 2010. Zebra. ISBN 9781420101768. 439pp.

Returning to the town of Reidsville, Colorado, Goodman adds a new resident to the charming town. Dr. Cole Monroe and his young sister Whitley have
left New York and come to the frontier. While making rounds, he stumbles
upon Judah Abbot's home, where he finds a bleeding, hurt, and scared Rhyne.
The town knows Rhyne only as Judah's son Ryan, or Runt as Judah calls him.
So begins Rhyne's rehabilitation and reentry into society as a woman. With
Cole's help, she comes to see that the lack of love given to her by her abusive,
cruel father is not the only type of love there is. A tempting tale of how love
can heal a broken spirit.

James, Judith.
Broken Wing. 2008. Medallion. ISBN 9781933836447. 440pp.

During the Napoleonic era, Gabriel St. Croix was abandoned as a child and
raised in a brothel. He has no family, no friends, nothing save Jamie, a young
boy who is brought to the brothel. Gabriel is determined to not let the same fate
happen to Jamie, and he protects Jamie with his own life and body. Sarah Mun-
roe hasn't stopped looking for her younger brother, Jamie, who disappeared
five years ago. Her dedication pays off, and he is found living in a brothel in
Paris. Jamie has no memory of Sarah or the older brother who accompanies
Sarah. He refuses to leave the brothel without Gabriel. An agreement is made,
and Gabriel travels to a country estate, where he is a paid companion of Jamie.
Gabriel's transition to freedom is difficult. He suffers from what we would now
call posttraumatic stress disorder and to ease the pain he often cuts himself.
Sarah can't stand seeing him suffer and works to bring him out of his shell.
Over the course of many months, they find themselves falling in love. Gabriel
feels unworthy of Sarah's love and sets out to make his own way and prove
to her that he is worthy. Adventure and danger are ahead for both Gabriel and
Sarah, who, despite their separation, remain true to one another. A stunning
historical romance debut by James.

Jordan, Sophie.
How to Lose a Bride in One Night. 2013. Avon. ISBN 9780062033017. 372pp.

Annalise is not the catch of the season: She has a limp from a childhood
injury; she stumbles and is slightly overweight, but with her father's extremely
generous dowry, she is an attractive bride. Enough of a dowry to secure a marriage to the Duke of Bloodsworth. Sadly the duke has married Annalise only
for her money, and on their wedding night, instead of deflowering her, he attempts to murder her and dumps her body over the side of their wedding barge.

Luckily for Annalise, she survives and is found washed up on the riverbank by Owen. He brings her to a gypsy healer, who sets her leg and allows her to rest. While she is recuperating, she is hesitant to get to know Owen as she is terrified that her murderous leech of a husband will reappear. Owen is working through his mental anguish dealing with the atrocities of war, but time spent together breeds familiarity and the two establish a tentative friendship. When the duke does find Annalise, Owen is there to protect her and together they save the day and each other.

Joyce, Brenda.
The Perfect Bride. 2007. HQN Books. ISBN 9780373772445. 377pp.

Blanche Harrington has shut herself off from any great emotions. She doesn't feel passion, pain, love, or happiness; she simply is. Her mother is long dead, and her father recently died, leaving her a vast fortune that needs a husband to manage it. Word has gotten around about Blanche needing a husband and too many suitors are calling. She flees to the countryside to visit Sir Rex de Warenne, the brother of a former suitor with whom she has always gotten along. Catching Sir Rex, the war hero who lost a leg in the Napoleonic war in a very delicate situation with a housemaid, may have caused another woman to pack her bags and return home. Blanche and the dark, brooding Sir Rex come to spend enough time together that they find themselves attracted to one another and pursue an affair. Blanche begins to have horrible flashbacks to the night when her mother died and fears she is going mad. Sir Rex gently helps her deal with her fears and works through her nightmares to uncover what really happened. This is a tale of not one but two wounded souls coming together to forge a love that will heal them both.

Jump, Shirley.
The Sweetheart Bargain. 2013. Berkley. ISBN 9780425264508. 304pp.

After inheriting a house in Rescue Bay, Florida, from the birth mother she never knew, Olivia Linscott leaves Boston for a fresh start. She arrives to find a house in dire need of repairs and Diana, a sister that she knew nothing about. An injured dog in her backyard leads to a meeting with Luke, the hot but physically and emotionally scarred Coast Guard pilot who lives next door. Luke has a lot of baggage stemming from the accident that injured him and killed his best friend. Olivia's job as an animal-assisted therapist introduces her to the Sweetheart Sisters, three meddling senior women led by Luke's grandmother who decide that Luke and Olivia would be perfect for each other and do their best to make it happen. A heartwarming series debut that continues with Diana's story in *The Sweetheart Rules*.

Woods, Sherryl.
Beach Lane. 2011. Mira. ISBN 9780778329893. 360pp.

Susie O'Brien and Mack Franklin have been "just friends" for several years. All of their friends and family can see how right they are for each other, but Susie is afraid to take the relationship further because Mack has always been a player. Mack has finally decided to propose when he loses his job. Having grown up in a dysfunctional family, he doesn't think it would be right to propose now that he has nothing to offer her. When Susie finds out that Mack has been keeping the loss of his job a secret from her, she is furious, but her anger is overshadowed by fear when she learns that she may have ovarian cancer. You'll need to keep the tissues handy during your visit to Chesapeake Shores, MD, but the O'Brien family will make you feel right at home. (Chesapeake Shores, #7)

Dangerous Attraction

Books on this list will keep you on the edge of your seat, waiting to discover what happens next.

Brennan, Allison.
▶ *Love Me to Death*. 2010. Ballantine Books. ISBN 9780345520395. 496pp.

Six years ago, Lucy Kincaid was raped and tortured before she was able to kill her kidnapper in order to survive. While waiting to find out if she will be accepted into the FBI Academy, Lucy volunteers for Women and Children First, an organization that monitors paroled sex offenders. A program Lucy created is being used to track down sex offenders and kill them, and now Lucy is getting the wrong kind of attention from the FBI. Her brother's partner, Private Investigator Sean Rogan, works with Lucy to discover how the murders are connected. Breakneck speed, sexual predators, and a sweet love story are all part of this creepy new series. While this is the first book in the Lucy Kincaid series, Brennan has written about the Kincaid siblings before in both her Evil trilogy and her FBI trilogy.

Griffin, Laura.
Untraceable. 2009. Pocket Star. ISBN 9781439149195. 374pp.

Computer expert Alexandra Lowell has her own private investigation firm in Austin, Texas, specializing in helping abused women disappear. She creates new identities for them and sets up false trails to throw off anyone who might come looking for them. One of her clients, Melanie Bess, was married to an abusive cop, and has recently become unreachable. When Alexandra discovers evidence of foul play, she brings her suspicions to homicide investigator Nathan Devereaux. With no body, Nathan is reluctant to become involved, but Alexandra persuades him to look further. She also enlists the help of "tracer" Mia Voss from the Delphi Center, a privately funded forensic lab. With a strong hero and heroine and a fast-paced plot, the romance grows as the story progresses. Alexandra and Nathan both made their first appearances in Griffin's Glass Sisters series, but Griffin provides enough backstory for all but the most hard-core series readers.

Martin, Kat.
Against the Fire. 2011. Mira. ISBN 9780778329305. 416pp.

    Gabriel Raines isn't about to let the recent outbreak of arson get to him but it is hard to not take it personally when his real estate projects seem to all be going up in smoke. Mattie Baker can't believe that Angel, one of the boys she works with at the community center, is responsible for the fires. Thrown together by their desire to find the real arsonist, sparks fly between Gabe and Mattie. If only Mattie would let herself enjoy what is developing between them. A good blend of suspense and romance. (Raines of Wind Canyon, #2)

Perini, Robin.
In Her Sights. 2010. Montlake Romance. ISBN 9781612181523. 262pp.

    When Jefferson County's SWAT team sniper "Jazz" Parker saves the governor's daughter, she draws unwanted attention to herself. Changing her name and reinventing herself while still a teenager, she has put a lot of effort into keeping her past hidden. Two years ago, she left the only man she ever loved, reporter and former Army ranger, Luke Montgomery, when she realized he was getting too close. Now his story has put her on the front page, and her former enemy returns with a vengeance. Jazz has never really trusted anyone, but in order to survive she needs to put her trust in Luke. A strong female character, sexy hero, and unrelenting action will keep you on the edge of your seat. (Montgomery Justice, #1)

Solomon, Annie. ♛
Blackout. 2006. Warner Forever. ISBN 9780446616317. 354pp.

    Waking up in the middle of the night, bookstore owner Margo Scott feels unusually disoriented; she can't remember anything that's happened in the last month. When the police arrive to question her about the death of Frank Temple, the deputy director of the Terrorism Control Force, she swears she's never met him, but they have a photo of Margo with Frank. Everyone close to her seems to have disappeared, she finds a secret stash of weapons, and she seems to have some unusual skills that she doesn't remember obtaining. Jake Wise, the hot undercover agent who has been tailing her, seems to be the only one who doesn't want her dead. Margo and Jake work together to uncover the truth in this riveting thriller with a slow, sexy romance.

Webb, Debra.
Traceless. 2007. St. Martin's. ISBN 9780312942229. 340pp.

    Ten years ago, Emily Wallace's best friend, Heather, was murdered in Emily's bed, and she found Clint Austin with blood on his hands. Her testimony put Clint behind bars. When she learns that Clint is being paroled, Emily comes home to Pine Bluff, Alabama, hoping to find a way to send him back to prison. Clint survived a lot in prison, but now that he's free, he's determined to find the real killer and prove his innocence, especially to Emily. As strange events start happening in Pine Bluff, Emily begins to wonder if she sent the wrong man to jail, but if Clint didn't kill Heather, who did? As they work together to discover Heather's murderer, the attraction between them heats up as they get closer and closer to the truth. (Less, #1)

Inspired By Love

These romances focus on religious values. Characters overcome adversity while adhering to a strict moral code. They may be struggling with their religious beliefs or have newly embraced them. There is little sex, profanity, or violence, but there are frequent references to the Bible.

Alexander, Tamera. ☗
Revealed. 2006. Bethany House. ISBN 9780764201097. 332pp.

Annabelle Grayson McCutchens and her husband Jonathan are on their way to a new life in Idaho when he dies just past Denver. She brings his body back to Willow Springs, Colorado, and advertises for a guide who can take her to their ranch. When Jonathan and Annabelle married, his brother Matthew Taylor was scandalized that Jonathan would marry a whore from a brothel, and after words were exchanged between them, he left Colorado. Matthew has just returned, hoping for a reconciliation and on the run from a bounty hunter. Matthew answers Annabelle's ad, and despite the issues between them, she hires him to be her guide. As they travel west, they learn to respect one another and trust in God's plan as they fall in love. (Fountain Creek Chronicles, #2)

Carlson, Melody.
A Mile in My Flip Flops. 2008. WaterBrook Press. ISBN 9781400073146. 336pp.

Less than four weeks before the wedding, Gretchen Hanover's fiancé dumps her. After 18 months of watching too much HGTV and consuming lots of Ben & Jerry's, Gretchen decides that she needs to move on. With her contractor-father's help, Gretchen will buy, renovate, and flip a house. Totally unprepared for all the things that can and do go wrong and with a tight deadline, Gretchen grudgingly accepts help from her father's carpenter friend. Noah Campbell is a gorgeous master carpenter, but he's also divorced and has a child. As they work together on the house, sparks fly between them. Gretchen's faith in God is restored as her house and her heart get a makeover.

Fisher, Suzanne Woods.
The Choice. 2010. Revell. ISBN 9780800733858. 308pp.

Carrie Weaver's plans to leave the Amish life and marry baseball player Solomon Riehl are changed by her father's death. She agrees to a marriage of convenience to get herself and her hemophiliac brother Andy out from under her stepmother's roof. Although Carrie doesn't love Daniel, she grows to love his family. They are both keeping secrets, from each other and from their community. But as time passes, their feelings for each other grow. Then tragedy strikes. Though not Amish herself, Fisher's grandfather was raised Plain, and she's been able to incorporate a lot of personal knowledge of the Amish ways into her writing. (<u>Lancaster County Secrets</u>, #1)

Hannon, Irene. ♟

▶ *In Harm's Way*. 2010. Revell. ISBN 9780800733124. 336pp.

When Rachel Sutton picks up the Raggedy Ann doll in a restaurant parking lot, she experiences a strange feeling of dread. Although she knows that she won't be taken seriously, Rachel brings the doll to Special Agent Nick Bradley of the FBI. Nick doesn't think she's crazy but doesn't plan to look into it any further until the story is picked up by the newspaper. Researching it further, Nick discovers links to a missing baby who may be connected to Rachel. Nick's interest in getting to know Rachel better and concern about her safety bring them together as they try to find out more about the doll and the missing child. Rachel and Nick both experienced difficult childhoods but have developed into strong characters, and the romance that develops between them is sweet and satisfying. Faith is important, but Hannon does not overwhelm the story or the reader with it. (<u>Heroes of Quantico</u>, #3)

Lewis, Beverly.

The Bridesmaid. 2012. Bethany House. ISBN 9780764209789. 316pp

After being in several weddings, Joanna Kurtz fears that she may be always the bridesmaid and never the bride. While attending a family funeral in Virginia Beach, she meets Eben Troyer, a fellow Amish from Indiana, and they begin a long-distance correspondence. Joanna dreams of being a published author and writes secretly in her journal. Eben longs to leave Indiana and move to Pennsylvania so that he and Joanna can marry, but unless his brother returns from the English world, his family needs him on the farm. Can the two find a way to have their own happily ever after? Lewis offers a fascinating depiction of the Amish way of life, with a leisurely pace, and quiet romance. (<u>Home to Hickory Hollow</u>, #2)

Witemayer, Karen.

To Win Her Heart. 2011. Bethany House. ISBN 9780764207570. 352pp.

In 1887, Levi Grant is looking to start over; he's served his time for accidentally killing a man in a boxing match and found God in the process. Levi has come to Spencer, Texas, to be the town's new blacksmith. Upon meeting the daughter of the town's founder, librarian Eden Spencer, Levi hopes for more out of life. Five years ago, Eden was jilted less than a week before her wedding; since then her only love is books. Due to his lisp, Levi is a man of few words, but a shared passion for literature brings them together. Is there hope for a future when Eden learns about his past?

It Was a Dark and Stormy Night:
Gothic Romances

Gothic romances are poised to make a comeback. These examples take the best of Victoria Holt, Mary Stewart, and Phyllis Whitney, and give them a modern (historical) twist.

Campbell, Anna.
Seven Nights in a Rogue's Bed. 2012. Forever. ISBN 9781455512072. 416pp.

When Jonas Merrick learned of her penchant for gambling, he came up with a plan to get revenge against his cousin and sworn enemy, Roberta's husband, Viscount Hillbrook. Jonas was going to ruin Roberta by making her spend a week in his bed. Arriving at the foreboding Castle Craven during a driving rainstorm, Sidonie Forsythe has come to pay her sister's gambling debt. Jonas, scarred and damaged emotionally and physically, is intrigued by the beautiful innocent and changes his plan—over the next seven nights, Sidonie is to be his guest. He will try to seduce her, but she will be free to leave at the end of the week, even if his attempts fail. A dark and steamy *Beauty and the Beast*, this is the first in the Sons of Sin series.

Coulter, Catherine.
The Prince of Ravenscar. 2011. Putnam. ISBN 9780399158070. 416pp.

Haunted by the death of his wife Lily three years ago, widower Julian Monroe, the titular Prince of Ravenscar, has finally returned home. His mother is excited to have him home and plans to take him to London for the Season. She'd like him to remarry and has already chosen his bride, Sophie Wilkie, the daughter of her dearest friend. Lord Devlin Monroe, Julian's nephew, accompanies them and becomes quite taken with Sophie's aunt and chaperone, Roxanne Radcliffe. Members of Lily's family still believe that Julian had a part in Lily's death, especially her brother Richard. Blending romance and mystery, a kidnapping, a fire, and a rumored vampire, the 11th book in Coulter's Bride series has something for everyone.

James, Samantha.
▶ *The Secret Passion of Simon Blackwell*. 2007. Avon. ISBN 9780060896454. 384pp.

After losing his wife and young son in a tragic fire, Simon Blackwell vowed never to marry again. For the past five years, he has lived a solitary life on his Yorkshire estate. A trip to London introduces him to Annabel McBride, and after a heated kiss between them is witnessed by Annabel's brother, they soon find themselves married. Simon plans to wait a decent interval and then divorce Annabel, but she hopes for a real marriage with children. Simon's guilt about the fire will break your heart. The atmospheric setting and hints at deep secrets in this emotional, sexually charged romance will keep readers turning the pages long after the lights should be out. (McBride Family trilogy, #1)

Klassen, Julie.
The Silent Governess. 2010. Bethany House. ISBN 9780764207075. 448pp.

When she sees her father strangling her mother, Olivia Keene hits him over the head with the nearest blunt object. Believing that she killed him and will be charged with his murder, Olivia runs away from home and ends up at Brightwell Court. She is discovered by Lord Edward Stanton Bradley after she overhears a conversation that could ruin him. Edward insists that she accept a position as governess and keeps her under his watchful eye. As they spend more time together, Edward discovers that Olivia has her own secrets. Klassen seamlessly weaves together romance, politics, and mystery in this compelling historical romance.

Medeiros, Teresa.
The Temptation of Your Touch. 2013. Pocket Books. ISBN 9781439157909. 432pp.

Maximillian Burke, the Earl of Dravenwood, has always been the model gentleman and a dutiful son, but after his intended leaves him at the altar to marry his brother instead, he decides that there is something to be said for being a rogue. After getting into a duel, he retreats to Cadgwyck Manor, the farthest flung property in the family holdings, located on the cliffs of Cornwall. He arrives to find a run-down estate that is said to be haunted and servants who seem to be determined to drive him from his home. Housekeeper Anne Spencer has been able to come up with a plan to rid the estate of previous occupants and is determined to do the same to Max. The servants are eager to go back to hunting for the Cadgwyck family treasure that is rumored to be somewhere on the estate. Max is equally determined to stay and to get to the bottom of the mystery surrounding the resident ghost, the White Lady of Cadgwyck. Anne and Max have both experienced heartbreak and scandal; their attraction to each other helps them to heal. This is the sequel to Medeiros's *The Pleasure of Your Kiss*, but it can be read as a stand-alone text as well.

Novak, Brenda.
Through the Smoke. 2013. Montlake Romance. ISBN 9781477808764. 316pp.

Bookseller Rachel McTavish lost her father and brother to the coal mines and has been fighting for better conditions for the men who are still risking their lives there every day in the 1840s England. Despite hating everything he stands for, she makes a deal with Truman Stanhope, Lord Druridge, to exchange the information she knows about his wife's death two years ago in a fire if he will send a doctor to save her dying mother. Truman had planned to divorce his wife after discovering she was pregnant with another man's child and can't remember the night of the fire, but he is sure that he never would have harmed Katherine. Rachel and Truman are falling for one another, but they have a lot to figure out before they can have a future together and Rachel's association with the earl has caused the town to turn against her. *Through the*

Smoke is Novak's return to historical romance, after years of writing contemporary romance. She breaks from some of the typical staples of the genre, but she makes it work. This is a compelling story with strong characterization and great chemistry between the hero and heroine.

Stuart, Anne.
Never Kiss a Rake. 2013. Montlake Romance. ISBN 9781477807323. 342pp.

After their shipping magnate father is accused of embezzlement and then is killed in a suspicious accident, Bryony Russell and her two younger sisters are orphaned, impoverished, and shunned by society. Bryony is determined to clear her father's name. She poses as a housekeeper when a position becomes open at the London residence of Adrian Bruton, the Earl of Kilmartyn. There is trouble in the household; the earl and the countess despise each other. The earl is said to be a womanizer, while the countess is unfaithful. Adrian is quick to realize that there is something off about the new housekeeper and is determined to find out what secrets she is keeping. Bryony has led a sheltered life due to the smallpox scars on her face and believes that she will never find a man. The first book in the Scandal at the House of Russell series is dark, atmospheric, and edgy. The tension and foreboding will hold the readers' interest, leaving them eager to see what is next for the Russell girls (hint: sister Madeline falls for a pirate).

Sizzling Hot Reads

Watch out, these steamy romances are HOT! Whether they are historical, urban fantasies, or contemporaries, the one thing these books have in common is sex. Lots of it and it is flaming hot! Not for the faint of heart. Erotic romance or sizzling reads have an emotional relationship between the hero and the heroine as the main focus along with a sexual relationship that is integral to the storyline. The happily ever after is standard for an erotic romance.

Arend, Vivian.
High Risk. 2013. Berkley Sensation. ISBN 9780425263334. 312pp.

Search-and-rescue climber Rebecca is dealing with the aftermath of a horrific climbing accident that claimed the life of her partner and lover, Dane. To keep herself busy, she accepts a job with an elite search and rescue team in need of motivation and training. This new job puts her directly in the path of an old lover she has never gotten over. Since their time together, Marcus has had his own demons to deal with. He lost part of one arm in an accident. Marcus uses sex and domination as a way of overcoming his feelings of inadequacy. Rebecca uses Marcus and sex to forget about the parts of the accident that she can't remember. Together they overcome their demons and forge a wildly hot relationship that burns up the pages.

Burton, Jaci.
▶ *Taking a Shot*. 2012. Berkley Heat. ISBN 9780425245521. 324pp.

When you have two brothers who are professional athletes and your family owns a sports bar that you manage, you might know a bit more than most females about sports, but for Jenna Riley it also means that she doesn't want to date any athletes. Ever. Then Tyler Anderson, star hockey player, walks into her bar. Sexy, cocky, intriguing Tyler decides that he likes the tiny, tattooed, pierced bartender, even though she goes completely against his type. Their chemistry is felt right from the first chapter when Tyler steps in and helps her out during a rush at the bar and ends the night with a searing kiss that has her panties wet and her heart pounding. Jenna can only hold out for so long before Tyler works his way into her bed. As their friends–with-benefits relationship continues, Jenna is not shy about telling and, in some cases, showing Tyler what she likes in bed. Outside the bedroom, Tyler encourages Jenna to reveal the real reason she hates sports to her family. Jenna realizes that she can date and maybe even love an athlete, as long as that athlete is Tyler. (Play by Play, #3)

Dane, Lauren.
Coming Undone. 2010. Berkley. ISBN 9780425232705. 291pp.

Former ballet dancer Elise Sorenson has moved to Seattle, Washington, from New York with her young daughter to escape the past, including a bad marriage. She is looking for peace, quiet, and, most certainly, not love or romance. She had the bad fortune to move across the street from sexy, tattooed, biker boy Brody Brown. Brody is now on his own after raising his two younger siblings after their parents were killed in a car accident. When Brody is hit by a car, Elise comes to his aid and thus begins their tender journey from friends, to friends with benefits and finally to more. Tender in affection and romantic with words, Brody is swoon worthy and when they get down to business in the bedroom, and the ballet studio and the tattoo shop Brody owns, things get downright steamy! Dane has a knack for making you care about everyone in the town, not just the main characters. Secondary characters from the previous book in this series are revisited, and we are treated to a ménage scene that will have you reaching for a cold drink.

Hayes, Jasmine.
The Naughty Corner. 2013. Berkely. ISBN 9780425266236. 320pp.

Babysitting her twin nephews while their parents travel through Europe is not Lola Cook's idea of fun, but she is trying to make the best of it. To get the teen troublemakers out of her hair so she can meet her writing deadline, she enrolls them in football camp. Lola knows they are difficult, but she never expected them to almost be thrown out of football camp. Coach Gray Barnett is intent on kicking William and Harry out of his camp. Then he meets their aunt and has a better idea. Each time the boys misbehave, Lola will take their punishment. In private. Lola isn't looking for a relationship, she's been in a bit of a dry spell and Coach Gray is attractive, sexy, and single, so why not? They engage in a highly sexual affair with the coach delivering various manners of punishments to Lola. Punishments range from spanking to dirty talk, oh the dirty talk, and more. Lola willingly accepts the punishments and now and then turns the deal upside down and hands out a punishment or two to the coach. Soon enough the two realize that this is more than just fun and games; they are both falling for each other and hard. It takes a while for them to figure out what to do since neither of them wanted a relationship.

Hill, Joey W.
In the Company of Witches. 2012. Berkley. ISBN 9780425250846. 329pp.

Raina, part witch and part succubus, runs a bordello of the demon kind. She specifically houses other incubi and succubi and offers them protection. That protection doesn't always sit well with the powers that be. When Isaac, an incubus, shows up with something he stole from Lucifer, all hell is about to break loose. Underworld Dark Guardian Mikhael is on a mission to retrieve it. He shows up at Raina's business and refuses to leave without it. In between arguing and getting on each other's nerves, a raw intense attraction flares between Mikhael and Raina. Acting upon that attraction, they begin a passionate affair in the midst of a battle between light and dark that puts Raina's life in danger. Mikhael is determined to protect her at all costs. He can't lose her now that she has broken down his defenses and worked her way into his heart. (Arcane Shot, #2)

Holly, Emma.
Beyond Seduction. 2002. Jove. ISBN 9780515133080. 297pp.

Merry Vance, daughter of the Duke of Monmouth, does not want to marry. She especially does not want to marry the gentleman her mother has chosen for her. Desperate to find a way out, Merry comes upon the perfect scheme. She will pose nude for Nicholas Craven, one of London's most notorious artists. Surely no man will want to marry her after she has so boldly ruined her reputation, and she will be free to live her life as she chooses. What she didn't count on was Nicholas himself or the fierce attraction she feels for him. This isn't your grandmother's Regency romance! Their relationship begins as a very steamy sexual one and gradually morphs into something more.

Lynn, Cherrie.
Rock Me. 2011. Samhain. ISBN 9781609280802. 280pp.

Candace Andrews is done. She's had it with her overbearing, controlling family. They have chased away every man who has ever shown any interest in her. Her family has managed to keep her a virgin at 23. For her birthday, she is finally going to do something that pleases herself. Her birthday treat to herself is a tattoo from Brian Ross's tattoo shop—the same Brian Ross whom she had a major crush on when he was dating her cousin two years ago. Having his hands on her makes her want him all over again. She knows that her family will never approve of him, with his arm sleeves, piercings, and bad-boy attitude, but she doesn't care. With him she feels more like herself than she ever has. Brian is a tender and gentle bad boy but don't let that fool you; he knows what he is doing and how to use those piercings of his to their best advantage. Second in the Ross Siblings series.

Rosenthal, Pam. ♀
The Edge of Impropriety. 2008. Signet Eclipse. ISBN 9780451222305. 336pp.

The widowed Countess of Gorham, Marina Wyatt spends her days crafting romance novels largely inspired by the doings of the Ton. Unlike the heroines in her books, she does not believe in forever relationships; instead, she sets the Ton's tongues wagging by indulging in a string of affairs. Having just ended things with one lover, she isn't looking for another when the uncle of her broken affair, Jasper Hedges, comes to town. Something about the very proper, slightly graying Jasper intrigues Marina. They begin a heated passionate affair that very quickly turns to love for Marina. A well-researched, somewhat literary, and extremely sexy look at the not-so-proper side of Regency England.

Chapter Four

Language

Language usually deals with a writer's style, and it can be very hard to pin down as an appeal factor. Romance readers rarely ask for books with flowery language or poetic descriptions, though that may be part of what the reader is looking for. In the *Smart, Funny Women* list, readers will find plenty to laugh about, while *He Writes Romance* offers romances written from a very unique perspective—all of the authors are men.

Language can also refer to format and the books in both the *Love.com* and *K.I.S.S.* lists have different formats from the books on other lists.

Smart, Funny Women

Who says love has to be serious? These funny ladies will make you laugh out loud.

Acosta, Marta.
Happy Hour at Casa Dracula. 2006. Gallery Books. ISBN 9781416520382. 320pp.

What's a wanna-be writer to do when her ex-boyfriend is hosting a launch party for his newly published book? Go, of course. And, that is exactly what Milagro de Los Santos does. Not exactly over her ex, Milagro meets Oswald, who almost makes her forget about Sebastian. After indulging in a little make-out session with Oswald, Sebastian comes knocking and Milagro flees. Soon after, she becomes violently ill and oddly, the target of a kidnapping attempt by Sebastian. Oswald's family rescues Milagro and explains that she is now a vampire and for her own protection she must stay with them. This does not sit well with our feisty heroine. She fusses and puts up a fight until Oswald quiets her down. The dialogue between well-educated (a degree from Fancy University) Milagro and Oswald is razor sharp. A quick and entertaining take on the vampire romance. (Casa Dracula, #1)

Craig, Christie.
Divorced, Desperate and Delicious. 2007. Love Spell. ISBN 9780505527301. 325pp.

Lacy Maguire didn't plan on harboring a police officer on the run, but she also didn't plan on doing her Christmas cards in February, or to be continuing the family tradition of divorce. At least Chase Kelly, the police officer, is hunky. After being framed for murder, he's desperate to prove his innocence and his partner's corruption. All Lacy wants is to send out those damn Christmas cards and get on with her life. She might even give up her recent vow of chastity if Chase sticks around any longer. He's too delicious to pass up. Filled with zany secondary characters, the first book in the Divorced trilogy is fast-paced and steamy.

Coburn, Jennifer.
Reinventing Mona. 2005. Kensington. ISBN 9780752816408. 357pp.

Frustrated with her life and lack of romance, Mona Warren, 31, takes a buyout from her engineering company and some time off to reflect upon her life. Falling back on a sizeable inheritance, she determines that if only she could convince Adam, her straight-laced accountant that she is the one for him all will be right as rain. With that goal in mind, she takes the advice of her BFF Greta, the therapist, and hires the manliest man she can think of, Mike "the Dog" Doughterty, to help her. Mike writes an advice column for a local magazine from a man's point of view. He agrees and begins to help her with one crazy idea after another. In the meantime, Mona becomes friendly with Mike's sister, Vicki, the stripper who redecorates Mona's house in classic movie themes. As Mona moves through the process of finding herself, she realizes that although Adam is developing feelings for her, she is falling in love with Mike, Greta is falling in love with Mona, and Mike is falling in love with Mona. A screwball comedy-fest of love, one-liners, and classic movie bathroom décor.

Fenske, Tawna.
Believe It or Not. 2013. Sourcebooks. ISBN 9781402257186. 384pp.

Campy, contemporary fun! Violet McFinn never wanted anything to do with her hippy-dippy mom Moonbeam's psychic business and even moved from Portland, Oregon, to Portland, Maine, to put plenty of space between them. Violet is an accountant, but when her mom breaks several bones and needs to have surgery, she must suspend her disbelief and become the temporary psychic in residence. Drew Watson is one of the owners of the strip club and bar, which hosts exotic male dancers, next door. He doesn't believe in psychic powers either but has a talent for playing just the right song to help Violet with her customers' readings. Fenske combines strong chemistry with a sprinkling of Eighties music and lots of laughs.

Forester, Amanda.

▶ *A Wedding in Springtime.* 2013. Sourcebooks. ISBN 9781402271786. 416pp.

It was supposed to be her shining moment, but that horrid William Grant made Eugenia Talbot laugh . . . while being presented to the Queen! She is ruined! Feeling quite responsible, William Grant takes pity on Eugenia and helps soothe the Ton's ruffled feathers so she can snag a husband. That is not the end of Mr. Grant's generosity. He also includes Miss Talbot in wild-goose chases to avoid spies, meddling relatives, and, of course, romance. The one thing that he doesn't want to do is find the charming, intelligent Eugenia a husband. He wants to be that husband. Forester keeps track of the many subplots and over–the-top characters with aplomb. (Marriage Mart, #1)

MacAlister, Katie.

Time Thief. 2013. Signet. ISBN 9780451417428. 341pp.

Kiya Mortenson's luck seems to have run out. She's got no job, her apartment building is being torn down, and she was just struck by lightning—for the second time—but she's still got a positive attitude and Eloise, her not-so-reliable 1969 VW bug. When Eloise breaks down, she meets the Faas and gets a job of babysitting five pugs in the Oregon Wilderness. The Faas are travellers. Travellers move from place to place, living by their own rules, much like gypsies; however, they also have the ability to steal time from humans, but they must pay for it or face the consequences. She meets Peter Faa when he is investigating a murder that he thinks was committed by a member of his estranged family. Peter and Kiya are polar opposites, but that doesn't stop the attraction between them. MacAlister is known for her fast-paced romantic comedies, and this doesn't disappoint. The witty dialogue keeps the story moving and pugs—who doesn't love pugs? First in the Travellers series.

Wilde, Lori.

You Only Love Twice. 2006. Forever. ISBN 9780446615167. 344pp.

Marlie Montague writes the popular *Angelina Avenger* comics. Angelina, unlike her creator, kicks butt and takes names defending the innocent against aliens and evil galore. Marlie never expected to get caught up in an Angelina-ish escapade, but she didn't expect a gun to be pointed at her head either! Luckily for her, her neighbor, whom she runs to for help, is hunky and handy with a gun, Navy secret agent Joel Hunter. Together they embark on an adventure that has Marlie realizing that she is more like Angelina that she thought. Joel is trying to keep them alive, but he can't keep his hands off her. A witty, madcap adventure with nods to the most famous spy that will have you laughing and cheering all the way.

Love.com

The Internet has complicated love in the 21st century. Twitter, Facebook, chat rooms, and e-mail have a big part to play as these couples find their own match dot com.

Bevarly, Elizabeth.
You've Got Male. 2005. HQN Books. ISBN 9780373770687. 384pp.
> Two years in prison for releasing a computer virus have made computer genius Avery Nesbitt agoraphobic, and eight years later, she only leaves her Manhattan apartment to take her cat to the vet. When you don't leave your house, it's tough to find love, but Avery thinks she's found the one until she discovers that Andrew has been cheating on her in other chat rooms. Top secret OPUS (Office of Political Unity and Security) agent Dixon has been trying to catch Andrew (aka the Sorcerer), a fellow agent who went rogue, for years and believes that Avery is the key to making that happen. Although she has been estranged from her family since her conviction, OPUS believes that the only way to keep her safe is to return her to her family home. Avery and Dixon fall for each other as they work together to catch Andrew. An original storyline, fast pacing, and a secondary romance between Avery's older sister and a junior agent 15 years younger all add up to one great read. (OPUS, #1)

Hunter, Denise.
Seaside Letters. 2009. Thomas Nelson. ISBN 9781595542601. 336pp.
> Sabrina takes her honeymoon alone in Nantucket after discovering that her fiancé cheated on her. Falling in love with Nantucket, she decides to stay—waiting tables in the morning and doing research for a local mystery writer in the evening. In an online chat room, Sabrina meets and falls for a local man, and is horrified when he turns out to be a regular at the cafe. She's done some things she's not proud of and knows that Tucker could never forgive her if he knew. Tucker discovers that Sabrina is his Sweetpea, but instead of confronting her, he hires her to track down his Internet pen pal. A beautiful love story about the power of forgiveness and God's love.

Kent, Allison.
The Icing on the Cake. 2010. HCI. ISBN 9780757315350. 264pp.
> By the time Michelle Snow turned 30, she still hadn't met her match. At the urging of friends, she signs up online with one of the popular dating sites and "meets" Todd Bracken. They live in different cities, but when they finally meet, they feel an instant connection. There isn't a lot of conflict here. Todd supports Michelle's dreams, and when she loses her job, he encourages her to open her own cupcake bakery. Kent's book is part of the True Vows series developed by the publishers of *Chicken Soup for the Soul*. Each book is based on the true story of a real couple. To find out more about

Michelle and Todd, check out their bakery's website at http://frostingacup
cakery.com/.

Meader, Kate.
Feel the Heat. 2014. Forever. ISBN 9781455599592. 416pp.

Curvy Lili DeLuca's meet-cute with British celebrity chef Jack Killroy
involves her in a painted on Wonder Woman Costume and him getting a
frying pan to the back of his head—not the best way to make a good first
impression, but sometimes you have to work with whatever comes your
way. Lili has put her career as a photographer on hold to take care of her
mother and the family restaurant after her mother is diagnosed with cancer.
Her sister Cara has arranged for Jack to go pots against pans with their
father in a televised cook-off that will boost Jack's career and, hopefully,
revive the flagging Chicago restaurant. When a video of Lili and Jack kissing goes viral, negative comments about Lili's weight are all over social
media. Jack loves Lili just the way she is, but can Lili learn to love herself
and Jack? Wonderfully witty dialog, steamy hot sex, and descriptions of
amazing dishes are only a few reasons to read Meader's strong debut. (Hot
in the Kitchen, #1)

Medeiros, Teresa.
▶ *Goodnight, Tweetheart.* 2010. Gallery. ISBN 9781439188156. 222pp.

Four years ago, Abby Donovan's debut novel was THE book of the year.
She's struggling to write her second book and feeling like she just might be a
one-hit wonder. To make sure that the public doesn't forget her, her agent has
signed her up for a Twitter account. An English teacher traveling the world
on sabbatical, @MarkBaynard, offers to be her personal guide to Twitter and
she quickly becomes his tweetheart. Can a relationship be built on 140 characters or less? Full of pop-culture references and told mainly through tweets,
Medeiros's only contemporary romance is delightful, heartbreaking, and
wonderfully fresh.

Park, Jessica.
Flat-Out Love. 2012. Createspace. ISBN 9781461085973. 400pp.

When college freshman Julie Seagle arrives in Boston for college, she
discovers that the apartment she rented over the Internet doesn't exist. Fortunately, her mother's college roommate offers to let Julie live with their family until she can find a new place. The Watkins' family seems to be almost
perfect—Erin and Roger are college professors; oldest son, Finn, is traveling
the world doing good works; middle son Matt goes to MIT; and 13-year-old
Celeste is quirky. Celeste has no friends and carries Flat Finn, a life-size card-
board cutout of her older brother, wherever she goes. Julie knows that something's not right, but no one will tell her what's going on. She turns to Finn
and through Facebook and e-mails, a relationship develops between them.
Parks has written a truly unique love story with a twist.

Impeccable Manners
and Formal Speech

Passion abounds but must be kept under cover. Romance within the rigid rules of society. Filled with historical details and a voice fueled by properness mixed with entendre, innuendo, and wit, these romances are a match for wordsmiths and history buffs alike.

Balogh, Mary.
▶ *At Last Comes Love.* 2009. Dell. ISBN 9780440244240. 386pp.

For Margaret Huxtable, one small white lie threatens to ruin her good name and her standing with the Ton. How could she have agreed to marry the infamous Duncan Pennethorn, the Earl of Sheringford? Because she was cornered by an old flame and afraid of being a labeled a spinster. For his part, Duncan is being held to a promise he made his cantankerous grandfather that he would be married before he turned 30. With barely a fortnight before then, can he charm and woo Margaret into marrying him despite his reputation? Maybe he could if his past didn't threaten to resurface at any moment and destroy their fledgling relationship. (Huxtable Quintet, #3)

Chase, Loretta.
Silk Is for Seduction. 2011. Avon. ISBN 9780061632686. 371pp.

Up and coming London dressmaker, Marcelline Noirotis is determined to make a success of the dress shop she owns with her two sisters. To make that happen, she heads to Paris to take in the latest fashions in hopes of using them to get the one large client from the Ton that the shop needs to become *the* destination for all fashionable members of society. While in Paris she meets the Duke of Clevedon. Knowing that he is heading back to London to finally marry his longstanding fiancée, Marcelline decides to convince him to persuade his fiancée to allow her to design her wedding dress. What follows is a slow dance of flirtation, seduction, and innuendo that, if allowed to go where it will, stands to end in disaster or, worse, scandal for them both. (The Dressmakers, #1)

Dare, Tessa.
Any Duchess Will Do. 2013. Avon. ISBN 9780062240125. 384pp.

Some Mothers will do anything to ensure that their children produce grandchildren for them. Griffin York's mother may have just outdone every other mother in her scheme to ensure grandchildren from her scoundrel of a son. She drugs and kidnaps him! She takes him to Spindle Cove and forces him to choose a woman that she will turn into the perfect mother of his children. Fed up with her scheming, he chooses a woman he is sure will never measure up to his mother's exacting standards and to the Ton's. He chooses Pauline, a serving girl. During the training period, where his mother tries to mold and shape Pauline into the proper London lady, he finds that he likes her just the way she is—A little sassy, strong, and, above all, all his. (Spindle Cove, #4)

Feather, Jane.
A Wicked Gentleman. 2007. Pocket. ISBN 978146525516. 480pp.

War widow Cornelia (Nell) and two of her lady friends travel from the countryside to London to inspect the home that was recently inherited by Lady Livia Lacey. Intending on staying for the season, they are shocked to discover that the house is ramshackle and practically falling apart. Determined to make the best of it, the ladies are pleased to make the acquaintance of Lord Bonham, who ensures them that he will introduce them to all of the fashionable ladies of society. By doing that, Lord Bonham will have the reasons and excuses he needs to be at the house. He is employed by the War Department and is on a mission to find hidden war secrets. If only finding the secret he is looking for was as easy as falling in love with Nell is proving to be.

Foley, Gaelen.
My Notorious Gentleman. 2013. Avon. ISBN 9780062075956. 360pp.

Grace Kenwood knows that she isn't in the same league as her handsome, charming neighbor, Lord Trevor Montgomery. She is a pastor's daughter, proper, kind, selfless, and everything that he is not. While the townspeople might view him as a hero, he sees only a jaded rake. Trying to win Grace's heart forces him to see that he isn't nearly as jaded as he thought he was or an incapable of love. (The Inferno Club, #6)

Hawkins, Alexandra.
After Dark with a Scoundrel. 2011. St. Martins. ISBN 9780312381264. 292pp.

One stolen kiss from Lord Dare and Regan's brother and protector sends her away to boarding school to protect her reputation and to educate her in the ways of a proper lady. Five years later, she returns home all grown up and quite the proper young lady. While she fully intends to impress the Ton, she has one goal in mind that definitely will not sit well with the Ton . . . seducing Lord Dare. She is determined to win him back and indulges in a game of wits with the man whom she has dreamed of every night since their stolen kiss. For his part, Lord Dare has tried to forget the girl he kissed, who happens to be the sister of his best friend, but he can't. Distance has indeed made his heart grow fonder. In a game of seduction where both parties are willing participants, is there really a loser or simply two winners? (Lords of Vice, #3)

Heath, Lorraine.
She Tempts the Duke. 2012. Avon. ISBN 9780062022462. 355pp.

Sebastian Easton, the Duke of Keswick, has not had an easy life. Kept against his will along with his younger brothers by his mad uncle, he has sworn to do two things. One is to reclaim his family's land, and the other is to reunite with Mary, his childhood friend and savior. Scarred and battle fatigued, he is heartbroken to find Mary engaged to a man who she doesn't love. Mary remembers well her childhood friend and sees past the scarring and the hurt to the passion that lies underneath. (Lost Lords of Pembrook, #1)

Hoyt, Elizabeth.
Wicked Intentions. 2010. Grand Central. ISBN 9780446558945. 392pp.

Accustomed to the finer things in life, Lord Caire hires widowed Temperance Dews to help him explore London's seamier side. He is determined to find the killer of his mistress. She is determined to find a patron for her family's orphanage. If she helps him, he will introduce her to the wealthiest women of London. If Temperance can push past the rumors and whispers that plague the duke about his sexual proclivities, she will see the man he really is. Together they discover more than a killer; they discover each other and their deepest secrets. More than that, they discover a deep, slow passion within. Suspenseful and sensual. (Maiden Lane, #1)

MacLean, Sarah.
One Good Earl Deserves a Lover. 2013. Avon. ISBN 9780062068538. 373pp.

With just a few weeks to her wedding, Lady Philippa (Pippa) Marbury realizes that her knowledge of the marriage bed is sorely lacking. Being of a scientific nature, she decides to conduct an experiment. She will enter into an agreement with a man to teach her what she needs to know. Pippa engages Cross, a partner at a notorious gaming hall, to be her research associate. Cross not only teaches Pippa about the mechanics of the marriage bed, but also about the sweet dance of seduction and temptation. Along the way Cross comes to see past Pippa's oddness and quirks to the gentle, sexy, very seductive woman she is. (Rules of Scoundrels, #2)

Quinn, Julia.
The Sum of All Kisses. 2013. Avon. ISBN 9780062072924. 384pp.

Outspoken, dramatic, and tenacious, Lady Sarah Pleinsworth is still annoyed at Lord Hugh Prentice for causing her beloved cousin Daniel to be forced into exile. In her eyes, it was Lord Prentice's fault for causing the duel that left Daniel in exile and the good lord with a crippled leg. One cannot forget that this little stunt caused her to miss her season. The shame! The horror! Now at 21, she is furious when circumstances throw them together and force them to be nice to one another. When they are not sparring and hurling insults, they are sneaking kisses and whispering sweet nothings. It all adds up to a fun and often laugh-out loud funny Regency. (Smythe-Smith Quartet, #3)

K.I.S.S.: Keep It Short and Sexy

When you're looking for something quick to read, reach for one of these e-novellas. Most of them are self-published, but they're all widely available online.

Aleo, Toni.
Falling for the Backup. 2013. Loveswept. ASIN B00CVS2KH0. 112p.

Nashville Assassins goalie, Jordan Ryan is trying to figure out what's next after a devastating knee injury. He meets Aynslee Shaw when he spills coffee on her as she's settling into the seat next to him on the plane to Nashville. Having to leave her niece's wedding to take care of an emergency at home, Anyslee is dressed in a hideous pink bridesmaids dress and hooker heels when she meets the hottest guy she's seen in a long time. Back in Nashville, their paths continue to cross, but how can they start a relationship when he's moving out of Nashville, just as she's settling in? (Assassins, #3.5)

Day, Nicolette.
No Strings Attached. 2013. Entangled: Flirt. ISBN 9781622661794. 45pp.
　　　Throwing caution to the wind, Hayden Summers decides that a wild night of anonymous sex is just the thing to erase the memory of her cheating ex. She's leaving tomorrow for her new job taking pictures for *Time* abroad. Jace Jennings, Hayden's best friend, has been in love with her for a long time. When Hayden and Jace are locked together in a storeroom, will he finally get the nerve to tell her how he feels?

Florand, Laura.
▶ *Snow-Kissed*. 2013. Laura Florand. ISBN 9780988506527. 122pp.
　　　After Kai's third miscarriage, her grief was overwhelming. She left her husband Kurt and has been holed up alone in an isolated mountain cabin. Kai is a food stylist and she has been working on a segment for her mother-in-law's magazine when Kurt shows up instead. Trapped together in the snow, they try to find a way back to one another. Steaming hot and so emotional, Florand has a gift for language and it is put to good use in this heart-wrenchingly beautiful story of loss and forgiveness.

James, Eloisa. ♛
Seduced by a Pirate. 2012. Avon Impulse. ISBN 9780062259912. 128pp.
　　　Unable to consummate his marriage to a beautiful older woman when he was just 17, Sir Griffin Barry ran away, got drunk, and was pressed into service on a ship headed to the West Indies. After 14 years as a pirate, he has been pardoned, returned to England, and plans to reunite with his wife Poppy. When he returns home, he discovers that while he was away, Phoebe (they'd known each other all of day before marrying and he'd gotten her name wrong) has had three children. After so long apart, Phoebe really isn't interested in giving their marriage another chance and suggests that they seek an annulment. Can Griffin change her mind? A follow-up to James's *The Ugly Duchess*.

Milan, Courtney.
The Governess Affair. 2012. Courtney Milan. ISBN 9781477591055. 101pp.
　　　After being raped by the Duke of Clermont, Serena Barton was fired from her governess position. Upon discovering that she is pregnant, she is determined to make him acknowledge what he's done and pay for his crime. Day after day, she sits on a bench outside his home. The duke sends Hugo Marshall, the "Wolf of Clermont," to deal with her. Hugo quickly realizes that there is more to the story than what the duke has told him. He doesn't respect the Duke but

is using him to obtain his goal to become "the richest coal miner's son in all of England." Hugo and Serena correspond from her position on the bench in short snarky missives sent back and forth as they each try to one up the other. Milan's novella is a touch dark, but it is a wonderful, witty introduction to the Brothers Sinister series. (Brothers Sinister, #0.5)

Rivers, Mary Ann.
The Story Guy. 2013. Loveswept. ISBN 9780345548740. 120pp.
   "*I will meet you on Wednesdays at noon in Celebration Park. Kissing only . . .*" When teen librarian Carrie West sees the ad on MetroLink, she's intrigued, and before she can overthink it, she responds. When she meets Attorney Brian Newburgh on Wednesday, she is totally unprepared for the hottest kiss of her life. It's clear from the start that Brian has a secret and that Carrie will ultimately do whatever it takes to discover what it is and to get more than just one hour a week with him. Powerful, emotional, and smoking hot.

He Writes Romance

Male romance writers are few and far between and often don't advertise that they're not women; they may hide behind gender-neutral names, use a pen name, or use initials instead of a first name. As long as the romance is convincing and has a satisfying ending, does it really matter who's doing the writing?

Buchman, M. L.
The Night Is Mine. 2012. Sourcebooks Casablanca. ISBN 9781402258107. 416pp.
   As the first female combat pilot to qualify for SOAR (the U.S. Army's Special Operations Aviation Regiment), Emily Beale has had to prove herself again and again. When she receives notice that she has been reassigned, she's horrified when she finds out what her new mission will be. An attempt was recently made on the First Lady Katharine Matthew's life. Katharine, having seen a CNN clip about Emily's abilities in the kitchen and in the air, has requested that Emily be assigned as her chef and bodyguard. Emily's commanding officer, Major Mark Henderson, is furious when he discovers what has happened to his best pilot. There's been a spark between them since their very first meeting, but he's never acted on it because fraternizing with a lower ranking officer could result in both of them being court-martialed. Offered a chance to pose as Emily's boyfriend while he works to discover who is behind the threats to the First Lady, Mark is using this opportunity to see if where there's smoke, there's fire. Combining action, adventure, and romance with humor and the politics of DC works well in the first book in the Night Stalkers series.

Coppernoll, Chris.
Screen Play. 2010. David C. Cook. ISBN 9781434764829. 342pp.

    The last year has been rough for Harper Gray; she's been unable to find a job and for her thirtieth birthday, instead of an engagement ring, her boyfriend told her he was moving to Los Angeles. When she's offered a chance to be an understudy for a revival of a classic play on Broadway, she leaves Chicago for a fresh start. She signs up for an Internet dating service, but her most promising match lives in Alaska. Her career is finally starting to take off—could God have a different plan in mind for her?

Greenwood, Leigh.
When Love Comes. 2010. Leisure Books. ISBN 9780843961362. 326pp.

    Broc Kinkaid was a rebel soldier during the Civil War; an ambush left his face damaged and scarred. When Broc breaks the jaw of a man who ridicules him, the judge who hears his case offers him a choice: collect on a debt for a widow who wasn't paid for a bull or go to jail. Wanting to stay out of jail, Brock visits the Liscomb ranch, where he meets the beautiful Amanda. Since her father died, she's been holding the family together and trying to make a success of the Lazy T. Amanda is unaware of a debt owed for the bull, and until the calves are big enough to sell, she can't pay it. Broc is willing to wait to collect payment and falls for Amanda, though he knows she could never love a man who looks like him. The romance builds slowly in this Western beauty and the beast. (Night Riders, #5)

Jordan, Wayne.
One Gentle Knight. 2007. Harlequin Kimani. ISBN 9780373860272. 288pp.

    The first in the Knight trilogy is eldest son, Shayne's story. After their parents were killed in a car accident, Shayne took over the family's sugar plantation in Barbados and raised his twin brother and sister, Russell and Tamara. When his siblings leave for college, Shayne accepts an invitation to spend a week in paradise. Carla Nevins has been living only half a life since her husband and unborn child were killed in the accident she survived two years ago; she hopes that her trip to Barbados will help her move on. Carla and Shayne are instantly drawn to one another, but when Carla wakes up alone, she wonders if it was just a one-night stand. After returning home to Virginia, Carla discovers that she's pregnant. She returns to Barbados to find out if they have a chance at something more. The beauty of the islands provides a lush background in this light, sexy romance.

Morgan, Jude.
An Accomplished Woman. 2009. St. Martin's. ISBN 97807755339037. 384pp.

    Turning down the county's most eligible bachelor, Lewis Durrant, 10 years ago scandalized local society, but Lydia Templeton has no complaints about the way things have turned out. Now 30 years old, she's fiercely independent and happy to no longer have to worry about affairs of the heart. When her

Godmother asks her to chaperone her ward, Phoebe, in Bath and help Phoebe to choose between the two gentlemen she's promised to marry, Lydia can't refuse. Arriving in Bath, Lydia finds herself running into Durrant everywhere she goes. Durrant is there to find a wife and he and Lydia wager fifty pounds over who will have more success in their missions. Although the ending is clear from the very beginning, Morgan delivers a satisfying read with just the right amount of wit and tension in this Austenesque Regency.

Murray, J.J.
The Real Thing. 2010. Kennsington. ISBN 9780758228871. 352pp.

Ten years ago, Dante "Blood and Guts" Lanza lost his last fight, but he's poised to make a comeback and hopes to win back his ex-wife at the same time. Magazine reporter Christiana Artis has been sent to Canada to interview him for a feature story on the sexiest men alive. When Christiana sees him, she makes a mental note to tell her editor that he needs to be moved much higher up the list. Dante doesn't do interviews but finally agrees to talk to Christiana if she does five things, including going fishing and a work out with him. Over the course of the next three days, they fall in love, but Dante is Italian and Catholic. He doesn't believe in divorce, and though he's tempted by the sexy, black reporter, he doesn't want to give up on getting his ex-wife back. Told from Christiana's point of view, we are treated to all of her internal thoughts in this sexy interracial romance.

Sheehan-Miles, Charles.
▶ *Just Remember to Breathe*. 2012. Cincinnatus Press. ISBN 9780988273603. 290pp.

Alex and Dylan first meet during a high school Ambassador Exchange trip to Israel. Living on different coasts, they struggle to make the relationship work while finishing high school. After a huge fight, Dylan enlists in the Army and is stationed in Afghanistan. Injured and dealing with posttraumatic stress disorder (PTSD), Dylan enrolls at Columbia and fate pairs him with Alex on a work-study assignment. Chapters alternate between Dylan's and Alex's points of view. Sheehan-Miles doesn't shy away from emotions or issues in this New Adult romance; the characters deal with class issues, substance abuse, and PTSD before getting their happily ever after. (Thompson Sisters, #2)

Fairytales Can Come True

For generations of women raised on princess movies and fairy-tale bedtime stories, these fairy tale–inspired reads are a welcome addition to the romance genre.

Boyle, Elizabeth.
Along Came a Duke. 2012. Avon. ISBN 9780062089069. 362pp.

The first book in the Rhymes with Love series opens with Tabitha Timmons living out a Cinderella-like existence in Kempton. Tabby, an orphan, has been left a fortune by her mother's estranged brother, but in order to collect it she must be married by her 25th birthday, which is just a month away. She learns that her uncle had picked out her husband and she is to travel to London to meet and wed a Mr. Reginald Barkworth. However, Tabby has fallen for Christopher Seldon, the Duke of Preston, despite his reputation for ruining young ladies. At the same time, Preston's family has determined that it is time for him to reform, and the best way to do that is for him to marry a respectable young lady from a good family. A colorful cast of secondary characters, flirtatious dialog, and a devoted Irish terrier with a penchant for feathers make this a delightful read.

Flinn, Alex.
Beastly. 2007. HarperTeen. ISBN 9780060874162. 304pp. Y A

Kyle Kingsbury has it all. Popular, handsome, wealthy, and a player. He's also mean, selfish, and arrogant. When he takes things too far and humiliates Kendra, a Goth loner, he finds out the hard way that she is a witch and cursed him to learn a lesson. She makes him as ugly on the outside as he is on the inside. Soon he is sporting fangs, fur, and claws. Confined to his family's brownstone, he spends his days growing roses, reading, and chatting online with other tragic heroes. His only hope of transforming back is to find true love. Nobody loved him before, and they certainly aren't going to love him now. Even his own father can't stand the sight of him. Kyle is alone, save a housekeeper and a blind tutor, until his Beauty arrives. A burglary at his home results in the burglar offering up his daughter to the Beast as his girlfriend in exchange for his own life. And so Lindy arrives to live with the Beast. Following closely to the originally fairy tale, Lindy begins to see the beauty in the Beast and he begins to believe that he has a chance at a normal life. Although readers know the ending, it is still heartbreaking to think that Kyle might not make the changes he needs to make in order to be changed back.

George, Jessica Day.
Princess of the Midnight Ball. 2009. Bloomsbury. ISBN 9781599903224. 280pp. Y A

Rose, along with her 11 princess sisters, is doomed to spend every night dancing with 12 princes in a secret chamber under their bedroom. Nobody, not even their father, the king, knows how they dance all night wearing out their dancing shoes but never leaving their locked bedchamber. Princes have come and gone, trying to observe them and find the secret to no avail. Until Galen, a young soldier, comes to the palace. Like so many before him, he falls in love with the beautiful Rose, but he is determined to find out the secret behind their dancing shoes. With some help from a few magical gifts he was given by an elderly woman whom he helped on his way home from war, he deftly solves the mystery and is rewarded with Rose's hand in marriage. An innocent take on the <u>Twelve Dancing Princesses</u> fairy tale with a prince who knits!

Gray, Juliana.
How to Tame Your Duke. 2013. Berkley Sensation. ISBN 9780425265666. 310pp.

    Fleeing Germany after her father is assassinated, Princess Emilie goes undercover as a tutor to Freddie, the son of the reclusive Duke of Ashland. The duke was wounded in India while fighting for the Crown. Soon after he returned, his wife abandoned him. The honorable duke is loyal to his wife's memory, loving no other but he is not above indulging in some dalliances with a companion at a nearby hotel. It just happens to be the same hotel that Emilie is staying at. When Ashland mistakes Emilie for one of his companions, they indulge in a steamy affair that has Emilie yearning for more. At the same time, a deep friendship develops as Emilie and the duke spend time together at his home. Of course, it isn't long before Emilie's true identity is discovered but that doesn't quell the passion between Emilie and the duke. The first in a trilogy featuring Emilie and her sisters.

Grayson. Kristine.
▶ *Wickedly Charming.* 2011. Sourcebooks. ISBN 9781402248481. 379pp.

    What happens when a fairy tale ends up not being so much of a Happily Ever After? Prince Charming discovers the hard way that you need to pick up the pieces and move on. Divorced from Cinderella and now living in the Greater World with his two daughters, he runs a bookstore and tries to keep a low profile, avoiding women and relationships in general. Mellie, stepmother to Snow White, has been exiled to the Greater World due to her alleged abuse of Snow White. Her organization PETA (People for the Ethical Treatment of Archetypes) is protesting at a local book fair when she meets Charming. He agrees to help her write a novel showing that stepmothers are not evil. Over the course of working on the book, Charming begins to agree that all stepmothers aren't evil, and their working relationship changes to friendship, and then to love. A sweet look at fairy tales and their endings. Part of the <u>Fates</u> series.

Hauck, Rachel.
Once Upon a Prince. 2013. Zondervan. ISBN 9780310315476. 352pp.

    Susanna was crushed when her boyfriend of 12 years broke her heart instead of proposing on the beach at St. Simon's Island. Her life is most certainly not going according to her plan. Adding insult to injury, her car breaks down at, of all places, Lover's Oak. In swoops Nathaniel to save the day. For Susanna and Nathaniel, the attraction is instant and intense. They begin to spend time together while Nathaniel is visiting distant family. Susanna is surprised when she accidentally finds out that Nathaniel is a royal prince! Royal duties and Susanna's insecurities about being in love with a Royal almost derail their relationship, but Susanna takes comfort in knowing in her heart that this must be God's new plan for her. A light, faith-based take on the Cinderella fairy tale.

James, Eloisa.
Once Upon a Tower. 2013. Avon. ISBN 9780062223876. 404pp.

Looking for a bride, Gowan Stoughton, the Duke of Kinross, attends the balls in London. He is a practical, well-mannered Duke looking for the same. He believes he has found that when he spots Lady Edith Gilchrist. He asks her father for her hand the very next day and just like that she is engaged to the Duke. Alas, Lady Edith was ill last evening and doesn't remember much of the ball at all, especially not the duke, who is now to be her husband. While arranging for the wedding, they embark on getting to know one another through letters. The duke is thrilled that he is going to be getting a wife who shares his sensibilities. When they are reunited before the wedding, a stolen kiss sets a flame a fire that the Duke didn't know he had in him. It doesn't take long before he is head over heels in love with Lady Edith. The path to true love is never straight . . . they marry, but they both come to the marriage bed innocents and that's when the trouble begins. Do they have what it takes to sort things out and put their marriage back together? Part of the <u>Fairy Tales</u> series.

Myles, Marina.
Beauty and the Wolf. 2013. Kensington. ISBN 9781601832108. 244pp.

After being cursed by his Gypsy grandmother, Lord Draven Winthrop turns into a werewolf with each full moon. The amulet Isabella Farrington received from her Egyptologist father curses her to kill her true love and commit suicide. Can these doomed lovers find love and happiness? <u>The Cursed Prince</u> series is continued by <u>Snow White and the Vampire</u>.

Chapter Five

Setting

Setting is not usually the key factor for readers in choosing a romance, but it can add that little extra something to a book. Readers looking to escape their life may enjoy reading something set in the West or reading about life in a small town. Who we are is influenced by where we are from, and certain areas may resonate more or less with readers. When setting is done well, readers feel like they are there with the characters, wandering the streets of a small town, traveling through time, or cooking with them in the kitchen.

Be My Valentine

What time of year is more romantic? Sugar and spice and everything nice to hot and steamy and very dreamy, these stories take place around Valentine's Day.

Crusie, Jennifer, Dahl, Victoria, and Stacey, Shannon.
Be Mine. 2013. HQN Books. ISBN 9780373777068. 392pp.
In Crusie's *Sizzle,* business and pleasure mix over an ad campaign for a hot new perfume called Sizzle. Dahl's *Too Fast to Fall* finds a deputy and a woman with a need for speed falling fast. The launch of a friend's restaurant reconnects a waitress with the one who got away after one perfect night together in Stacey's *Alone with You.* Crusie's story is the weakest, but it is interesting to read something from the beginning of her career and see how her writing style has changed.

Gibson, Rachel.
▶ *The Trouble with Valentine's Day*.2012. Avon. ISBN 9780060009267. 368pp.

Las Vegas private investigator Kate Hamilton heads to Gospel, Idaho, after her last case goes horribly wrong. She's stopped along the way by a blizzard and has one too many drinks in a bar. Although she's not that kind of girl; she decides a one-night stand with a sexy stranger might be just the thing to cheer her up on Valentine's Day. He turns her down flat. When she arrives in Gospel, her grandfather introduces her to the guy who owns the sporting goods store across from his grocery store. Naturally, he is the guy from the bar, Rob Sutter. A former hockey player, Rob has a bit of a thing about one-night stands after both his career and marriage are ended when he is shot by the stalker he picked up in a bar one night after a game. Then, the tables are turned and Rob can't think about anything but getting Kate in his bed, while Kate is looking for a commitment. A sweet secondary romance ensues between Kate's grandfather and Rob's mother. (Chinook's Hockey Team, #3)

Maynard, Janice.
Hot Mail. 2009. Signet Eclipse. ISBN 9780451225832. 274pp.

Jane Norman has had a thing for Ethan Oldman forever. They were best friends until Ethan's secret engagement broke her heart and ended their friendship. Several years pass and Ethan's engagement ends. Jane can't keep her feelings a secret anymore and decides to send Ethan sexy anonymous letters each week until Valentine's Day. A break-in at her stationery store brings Ethan, who is now assistant chief of police, back into her life, and he is suddenly seeing her in a new light. But will Ethan fall for Jane or his secret admirer? Smoldering sex scenes, a secondary older woman—younger man romance, and a little bit of suspense add up to a red hot read for Valentine's Day.

Ponti, Jamie.
Sea of Love. 2008. Simon Pulse. ISBN 9781416967910. 272pp. Ⓨ Ⓐ

Darby's father quits his Wall Street job right before her senior year of high school and moves the family to Florida to run the Seabreeze hotel. At first she hates Coconut Grove but, after making friends with Kate and getting to know surfing hottie Zach, Darby decides it isn't too bad. When her New York boyfriend shows up unexpectedly right before Valentine's Day, Darby has some tough decisions to make in this cute teen romance.

Michaels, Jess, Danes, Lacy, Hart, Megan, and Kessler, Jackie.
A Red Hot Valentine's Day. 2009. Avon Red. ISBN 9780061689390. 304pp.

For erotic romance readers who don't care what subgenre their romance is, this one's for you. Michaels give us a wicked little regency, Danes's offering is a hot historical, Hart writes a poetic contemporary, and Kessler's paranormal takes us to Hell and back. A great introduction to each of these writers, and, wow, does it sizzle.

Sands, Lynsay, Rush, Jaime and Palmer, Pamela.
Bitten by Cupid. 2010. Avon. ISBN 9780061894459. 384pp.

An anthology of paranormal romance stories featuring prolific author Lyndsay Sands and up-and-coming authors, Pamela Palmer and Jaime Rush. Sands's *Vampire Valentine* introduces mortal Private Investigator Tiny McGraw to Mirabeau LaRoche. Tiny is tasked with assisting Mirabeau in evading an enemy to deliver a package; Mirabeau is not too happy about having to travel through the New York City sewers in her bridesmaids dress. *Hearts Untamed* by Palmer focuses on Julianna from the <u>Feral Warrior</u> series. She's trying to protect everyone she loves from a secret in her past. This is made more difficult when her first love, Zeeland, returns 10 years after she last saw him. Rush's *Kiss & Kill Cupid* is paranormal suspense featuring Kristy, a character new to her <u>Offspring</u> series, who can hear other people's thoughts. During a job interview, she hears a serial killer who intends to make her his next victim. Is it her hot new boss Adrian?

Shope, Robin.
The Valentine Edition. 2009. Wild Rose Press. ISBN 9781601544841. 248pp.

In the second book of the <u>Turtle Creek</u> series, Jodi Williams leaves Chicago after a devastating betrayal. On her way to her new job at the *Turtle Creek* newspaper, she stops after almost hitting a dog. Before she can get to him, the next car coming past hits him. This leads her to veterinarian Josh Williams. There is an immediate attraction between them, but Josh's secretary Della Wheat has an obsessive interest in Josh and is determined to make him hers. The story takes place in the weeks leading up to Valentine's Day as Jodi helps plan the newspaper's first matchmaking Valentine's Day dance. Jodi's not sure she wants to stay in Turtle Creek, Wisconsin, but soon realizes that by putting her trust in God, she will end up in the place she's meant to be.

All I Want for Christmas Is You

There's no place like home for the holidays. While you're sitting in front of the fire and the snow is falling gently on the rooftops, read and enjoy one of these seasonal stories.

Adams, Noelle.
Married for Christmas. 2013. CreateSpace. ISBN 97814922765141. 205pp.

Good friends Jessica and Daniel are both missing something in their lives. For Jessica, getting married and having a family is the most important thing, while Daniel would love to move back home to Willow Park and be the pastor of their hometown church. But Jessica rarely dates, and the church elders aren't happy about the idea of a young unmarried pastor. Jessica proposes that they marry; she knows that Daniel has not gotten over his wife Lila's death two years ago and accepts that he will probably never love her. Full of heartbreak and hope, this is a sweet holiday romance. Although Daniel is a pastor, and spirituality and faith are important to the characters, the author very clearly states that this is a not an inspirational romance and there are several sex scenes.

Burrowes, Grace.

Lady Sophie's Christmas Wish. 2011. Sourcebooks Casablanca. ISBN 978140 2261541. 384pp.

Lady Sophie Windham just wants some time alone in London before all the hustle and bustle of Christmas. She has spent her life taking care of everyone else's needs and paying very little attention to her own. While waiting with a housemaid and her illegitimate baby for the arrival of a stagecoach, the maid runs off leaving Sophie with the baby. Sophie has a lot of experience with taking in strays but no experience with babies. Fortunately, Vim Charpentier comes to her rescue and offers to help calm the baby. Vim, believing Sophie to be a housekeeper, offers to accompany her home when a snowstorm hits and they are stranded for several days. As each day passes, Vim and Sophie fall more in love with each other and with young Kit. When Sophie's brothers show up to bring her to Kent, Sophie and Vim have still not discussed their true identities. Each believes the other to be of a much lower social station than their own, which means they'll never get their happily ever after. This is a spicy romance, and the baby gets considerable page time, so readers who prefer their romances clean and/or sans children should look elsewhere. While this is the first book in The Duke's Daughters series, readers who don't like to read out of order should be aware that it follows The Duke's Obsession trilogy, which is about Sophie's three brothers. (The Duke's Daughters #1)

DeStefano, Anna.

Christmas on Mimosa Lane. 2012. Montlake Romance. ISBN 9781612185873. 320pp.

This Christmas will be seven-year-old Polly Lombard's first without her mother, and she and her father Pete are both struggling with how to handle it. Mallory Phillips, the Lombard's new next-door neighbor, was hoping this Christmas would be different, but despite making a fresh start in Chandlerville, Georgia, she's still living a very solitary existence. As a child, Mallory spent most of her life on the streets; she's since become an elementary school nurse but still finds it difficult to let anyone get too close. When Polly starts visiting Mallory's house in the middle of the night to admire her tree, Mallory has to do something to help the grieving child, even if Polly's father would like Mallory to stay out of it. Through Polly, Pete and Mallory connect, and they all begin to heal. A sweet romance but one that will make you cry.

Jeffries, Sabrina.
'Twas the Night after Christmas. 2012. Gallery Books. ISBN 9781451642469. 368pp.

Pierce Waverly, the Earl of Devonmont, was sent away to boarding school at a very young age and has seen his mother only rarely since then. When he gets word that she is on her deathbed, he returns to his childhood home, hoping to discover why his parents virtually abandoned him as a child. He soon realizes that he has been tricked into coming home by his mother's companion, the beautiful widow, Camilla Stuart. He is convinced to stay but drives a hard bargain with Camilla—she will entertain him every evening that he stays. Camilla grew up an orphan and has been raising her son, Jasper, on her own since her vicar husband died. Family is so important to her and she can't imagine how Pierce can ignore his mother in the way that he has. Neither Camilla nor Pierce is what the other expected. Given his family situation, Pierce never expected to fall in love, but he'd never met a woman like Camilla before, either. Pierce, his mother, and Camilla all have their secrets; some are more surprising than others and will keep readers guessing until the end. Pierce and Camilla's story is just the thing for a cold winter's eve when the reader is nestled all snug in her bed. (Hellions of Hallstead Hall, #6)

Kaye, Laura.
North of Need. 2012. 212p. Gallery Books. ISBN 9781451642469. 354pp.

After losing her husband John two years ago on Christmas, Megan Snow still blames herself. Returning to the isolated mountain cabin where they'd spent so many happy days, she settles in to get through the holiday. Trying to take her mind off things, she goes outside to shovel snow and crafts a snow family, which only serves to remind her of all that she has lost. When she discovers a man unconscious on her doorstep in the middle of the blizzard, she drags him inside so he doesn't freeze to death. The man is Owen Winters, an elemental God of Winter who has been brought to life by her tears. Owen is an Anemoi, a weather god; only Megan's love can make him mortal. Just like Frosty the Snowman, their time is limited—they must fall in love before he melts away. Kaye uses the Greek myth of the Anemoi, Greek wind gods, as the basis of her sexy new paranormal series: Heart of the Anemoi; *North of Need* is book #1.

Lane, Katie.
Hunk for the Holidays. 2012. Hachette. ISBN 9781455522361. 352pp.

Cassie McPherson has no time for love. Knowing that her family will give her a hard time if she shows up for the company Christmas party without a date, she hires a male escort. When a gorgeous hunk in a tuxedo shows up at her office, Cassie assumes he's the date that she hired. James Sutton is amused that his biggest competitor's daughter assumes that he is an escort, but he's attracted to her and decides to play along. This is a departure from Lane's usual Cowboy fare—hopefully Lane will write about some of the other McPherson's in the future. Realistic family dynamics, humor, and hot sex make for a very Merry Christmas.

Morgan, Sarah.
Sleigh Bells in the Snow. 2013. HQN Books. ISBN 9780373778553. 384pp.

    Kayla Green has made a name for herself in public relations, at the expense of having a life and she likes it that way. The week between Christmas and New Year's is usually a hard one for her because the rest of the world is busy celebrating, but this year, she gets a chance at a new account. Snow Crystal Resort has been in Jackson O'Neil's family for four generations, and he wants to make sure it is still part of the family four generations from now. Kayla is invited to spend Christmas at the resort, so she can work out a marketing plan. The spark between Kayla and Jackson warms up the cold Vermont nights, and Kayla discovers that Christmas can be magical in this enjoyable seasonal romance.

Willig, Lauren. ♛
▶ *The Mischief of the Mistletoe.* 2010. Dutton. ISBN: 9780525951872. 340pp.

    The seventh book in the <u>Pink Carnation</u> series features Ms. Arabella Dempsey, a teacher at Miss Climpson's Select Seminary for Young Ladies and friend of Jane Austen. Arabella meets Reginald "Turnip" Fitzhugh when he visits to deliver a package for his sister Sally, a student at the school. A Christmas pudding with a mysterious note attached is the beginning of Arabella and Turnip's exciting adventures to save England while falling in love. While Willig's other books in this series are framed by the continuing story of Eloise Kelly, a modern day PhD student researching Regency era spies, this one is missing Eloise, perhaps because the time period covered in this one has already been explored in the fourth and fifth books.

Small Towns

Living in a small town is a lot like living with a very large extended family: the good, the bad, the ugly, and the sexy.

Blake, Toni.
One Reckless Summer. 2009. Avon. ISBN 9780061429897. 370pp.

    Good girl Jenny Tolliver has given up many of her dreams to do the "right thing." After her husband cheats on her with her teaching assistant, she returns to her hometown of Destiny, Ohio. An amateur astronomer, she runs into bad boy Mick Brody when she goes stargazing on the hill. An intense sexual affair begins between the two of them but Jenny knows that Mick is hiding something. Learning what it is puts Mick in danger and strains Jenny's relationship with her police chief father. (<u>Destiny</u>, #1)

Bretton, Barbara.

▶ *Just Desserts*. 2008. Jove. ISBN 9780515144246. 320pp.

New Jersey bakery owner and single mom Hayley Goldstein is shocked when lawyer Finn Rafferty asks her to make a cake for rocker Tommy Stiles's concert in Atlantic City. Hayley is flattered and knows the publicity will do wonders for her business. She doesn't suspect that the real reason she's been asked is to help Finn find out more about Hayley, who might be Tommy's daughter. Hayley's mother Jane, a well-known oceanographer, told Hayley that she used a sperm donor to conceive. The more Finn learns out about Hayley, the more he wants to know. A sweet secondary romance and a small New Jersey town are a big part of this Cinderella story.

Freethy, Barbara. ♕

The Way Back Home. 2012. Pocket Books. ISBN 9781451636550. 384pp.

Alicia Hayden and her family have a white-water rafting business in River Rock, a small town in Northern California. It's been in the family for years, but a recent accident that resulted in the death of her best friend's fiancé has put the business in jeopardy. Then only six days before his discharge from the marines, her twin brother Rob is killed. Rob's friend Gabe Ryder promised him shortly before his death that if anything happened to Rob, Gabe would help the family out. Gabe and Alicia had a one-night stand a few years ago, and while he's the last person she wants to see right now, she can't deny that she still finds herself drawn to him. Freethy's story is fast paced and will tug at your heartstrings, while the touch of mystery will keep you guessing until the end.

Gregory, Jill.

Sage Creek. 2011. Berkley. ISBN 978042524470. 304pp.

Finding out that her husband was cheating on her was bad enough, but finding out that his girlfriend is pregnant was devastating. Sophie McPhee leaves San Francisco and returns home to Lonesome Way, Montana. The diner is closing and Sophie decides it would be a good location for her new bakery, A Bun in the Oven. She doesn't want to have anything more to do with men, but after seeing her old crush Rafe Tanner again, she's having second thoughts. Rafe's wife abandoned him and their daughter a few years ago, and he's been raising her on his own ever since. The love story takes a while to progress because they are both wary about jumping into something new. The first book in the <u>Lonesome Way</u> series is a great introduction to the characters and town.

Roberts, Sheila.

Better than Chocolate. 2012. Harelequin Mira. ISBN 9780778313458. 400pp.

After her stepfather Waldo's death, Samantha Sterling takes over as head of Sweet Dreams Chocolate Company. Unfortunately, Waldo made more than a few questionable decisions and the new bank manager, Blake Preston, will not extend their loan. With the help of her grieving mother and two younger sisters, Samantha puts together a chocolate festival. But will it bring enough tourism to Icicle Falls, Washington, to raise the money to pay off the loan? Is anything better than chocolate? Find out in this sweet romance. Includes chocolate recipes. (Life in Icicle Falls, #1).

Stone, Juliana.
The Summer He Came Home. 2013. Sourcebooks. ISBN 9781402274800. 384pp.

Cain, Mac, and Jesse and his twin brother Jake were the Bad Boys of Crystal Lake. They've all returned to the tiny town in Michigan for Jesse's funeral, and they're each struggling with demons. Bad boy rocker Cain Black's marriage was a train wreck, which ended when he learned that his songwriting partner slept with his ex-wife. Maggie O'Rourke has come to Crystal Lake to escape an abusive relationship and start fresh with her 7-year-old son Michael. Cain was only supposed to be home for a few weeks, but the more he gets to know Maggie, the longer he wants to stay. Maggie doesn't want another relationship but seeing Cain with Michael breaks down her barriers. Humor is used effectively as a contrast to more serious issues, and the secondary characters add depth to the story. Stone balances Michael and Maggie's romance with Cain, Mac and Jake's renewed friendship, which sets up the next book in the trilogy, *The Christmas He Loved Her.*

Wiggs, Susan.
Winter Lodge. 2010. Mira. ISBN 9780778328919. 416pp.

Food columnist Jenny Majesky is still mourning the recent death of her grandmother when her house burns down one winter night and she loses everything except the bakery she inherited. Jenny, who has a long history with Rourke McKnight, Avalon's police chief, agrees to move in with him while she figures out what to do next. Interesting secondary characters and an appealing small-town setting combine in this sweet contemporary romance with just a little mystery. This is the second of nine books (so far) in Wiggs's Lakeshore Chronicles series. Tempting recipes for Polish baked goods are included.

Romancing the Stove

Great food is like great sex. The more you have, the more you want.
—*Gael Greene*

Food and story have been entwined ever since Eve ate the forbidden apple. Culinary romances prominently feature food or cooking; characters may be chefs, bakers, restaurant critics, or involved with food in some other way. Some of the books even include recipes for the dishes described.

Carmichael, Kathy.
Hot Flash. 2009. Medallion Press. ISBN 9781934755037. 325pp.

Jill Morgan Storm, a sous chef at a casino in Las Vegas, has more than her fair share of problems: Her ex-husband became a woman, her mother keeps trying to fix her up with unsuitable men, her professor boyfriend dumped her for a skillet-stealing college student, and she's trying to figure out how she's going to pay her son's art school tuition next year. On her 40th birthday, Jill declares that she is through with love, but her friends help her come up with a survey to send to the female half of couples who are featured in the local newspaper celebrating anniversaries of 25 or more years. After learning that the majority of these women have husbands who are rarely home, Jill decides that a traveling salesman is her best bet for finding true love and someone to pay the tuition bills. There's only one problem—Davin Wesley, her son's former teacher, seems to be constantly hanging around. The sparks fly between them, but how can it work when Davin's always at home?

Edwards, Louisa.
Can't Stand the Heat. 2009. St. Martin's Paperbacks. ISBN 9780312356491 368pp.

After receiving another rejection for her book proposal, sharp-tongued restaurant critic Miranda Wake might have had just a little too much to drink at the open house for Chef Adam Temple's hot new Manhattan restaurant, Market. She accepts his challenge to spend a month working behind the scenes, thinking it will help get her book published, but the publishers aren't interested in the serious book Miranda wants to write. Believing that Adam is nothing more than a pretentious fake, Miranda sets out to write a sleazy tell-all about him and his staff. Things heat up between them when Adam teaches her to cook, and Miranda is torn between her feelings for Adam and her need to finance her younger brother Jess's college tuition. The first of six books (so far) in the Recipe for Love series, *Can't Stand the Heat* is packed with authentic behind-the-scenes details, hot sex, quirky characters, and a sweet secondary gay romance that develops between Sous Chef Frankie and Miranda's brother Jess.

Hiestand, Heather.
The Marquess of Cake. 2013. Kensington. ISBN 9781601831293. 254pp.

Alys Redcake grew up working in her father's factories and is happiest when she's decorating cakes at Redcake's Tea Shop and Emporium. Michael is a frequent visitor to Redcake's, as he has a condition that causes him to feel shaky when he goes for several hours without eating and he has a fondness for sweets. Alys meets Michael, the Marquess of Hatbrook, when she serves him. After her father is knighted by Queen Victoria, her parents want to marry her off so that they can make better matches for her younger sisters, who have been brought up to be ladies. Circumstances seem to keep throwing Alys and Michael together, but can a baker and a Marquess find true love and happiness? This light, clever series starter brings up several thought-provoking points about history, economics, health, and the psychology of the times. (<u>Red-cakes</u>, #1)

Jump, Shirley.
   The Bride Wore Chocolate. 2004. Zebra. ISBN 9780821776919. 320pp.
   Before reading this frothy blend of romance and recipes, you had better stock up on chocolate and set your oven to 350 because you're going to want to bake along. There are only three weeks left until Candace Woodrow becomes Mrs. Barry Borkenstein. Everything that can go wrong does, including the dress shop burning down with her dress inside, the disc jockey having a heart attack, the priest running off with the transgender church secretary, but worst of all, Candace wakes up in another man's bed with a tequila hangover. Candace is a planner, which is why Barry, the accountant, is the perfect man for her. Can Michael convince her to take a chance on him before she says, "I do" to someone else? First book in the <u>Sweet and Savory</u> trilogy.

Kauffman, Donna.
   Sugar Rush. 2011. Brava. ISBN 9780758266347. 336pp.
   Leaving behind a successful career in New York City as executive chef at Gateau restaurant, James Beard's nominee Leilani Trusdale relocates to Sugarberry Island, Georgia, to be closer to her father and open her own restaurant, Cakes by the Cup. Lani's shop hasn't even officially opened when she finds out that her former boss Baxter Dunne, aka Chef Hotcakes, plans to film a week's worth of episodes for his hit television show in her cupcakery. While she secretly lusted after Baxter for years, she never dreamed that he had feelings for her; especially since he never did anything to squash the rumors about how she'd "earned" her position in New York. Lani and Baxter heat up the kitchen, but can they find the recipe for true love? Quirky secondary characters, steamy sex scenes, and two cupcake recipes make this a sure bet for readers looking for a light, fluffy treat. Followed by *Sweet Stuff* (2012) and *Babycakes* (2012).

Ockler, Sarah.
   Bittersweet. 2012. Simon Pulse. ISBN 9781442430358. 378pp. Y A
   On the most important night of her life so far, 14-year-old Hudson Avery finds out that her father has been cheating on her mother, and she blows her chance at becoming a professional ice skater. Three years later, her father is long gone and Hudson has hung up her skates. She is finishing her senior year and baking cupcakes for her mother's diner. She also secretly starts skating again. A chance for a scholarship has her coaching the varsity hockey team in exchange for ice time and brings her into contact with Josh and Will. The characters are well developed, and the situations are believable. Ockler showcases her witty dialogue and flawed, realistic characters in this sweet romance. Each chapter starts with a cupcake recipe. Yum!

Renwick, Sophie.
Hot in Here. 2009. NAL Trade. ISBN 9780451226914. 288pp.

Publicist Jenna McCade has had it bad for her former next-door neighbor, Bryce Ryder, ever since they were teenagers. After a magazine misquotes the celebrity chef, Bryce hires Jenna to do some damage control. After dinner in his restaurant, Jenna's birthday wish comes true when the two wind up having scorchingly hot sex. Knowing that Bryce will only break her heart, Jenna pretends that it meant nothing to her, but Bryce has begun to see her in a new light. Trust, honesty, and insecurity are issues for these characters, and they have to resolve them before they can try to make a relationship work.

Thomas, Sherry.
Delicious. 2008. Bantam. ISBN 9780440244325. 432pp.

When Bertie Somerset unexpectedly drops dead at the age of 38, his estranged, illegitimate half brother, Stuart, inherits his estate, which includes the legendary and infamous chef, Madame Verity Durant, Bertie's former mistress. Ten years ago, when it became clear that Bertie wouldn't marry her, Verity went to London to find Stuart and get her revenge on Bertie. Verity and Stuart spent one amazing night together, and Verity fell in love with Stuart but left without telling him her name. Now with Stuart engaged to be married, Verity must leave before he discovers that his new chef is the woman he hasn't stopped thinking about for the last 10 years. The descriptions of the food are evocative and erotic, the secondary romance is well plotted, and the sex scenes sizzle.

Usen, Amanda.
Scrumptious. 2012. Sourcebooks Casablanca. ISBN 9781402259821. 320pp.

Pastry chef Marly Bennet catches her best friend Olivia's husband Keith with his pants down in the cold room with one of the bartenders at Olivia's restaurant, Chameleon. After firing Keith, Olivia asks Joe Rafferty to be her temporary head chef before he moves to California to take a job as a celebrity chef. Marly and Joe both have a love 'em and leave 'em attitude toward relationships, but a couple of suspicious accidents in the kitchen have them pairing up to investigate. Usen's debut sizzles with steamy sex scenes, interesting details about restaurant life, and food descriptions that will leave you wanting to lick the page. The series is continued by *Luscious* (2012).

Down the Rabbit Hole

As if dealing with all the problems and difficulties of today's world aren't enough, these characters have a whole different time period to adjust to.

Anderson, Catherine.
Perfect Timing. 2013. Sourcebooks. ISBN 9780451239488. 422pp.

Quincy Harrigan has never been much of the romantic type or the believer in what he can't see. That is until the day he found Ceara O'Ceallaigh on his ranch. How she got there is a tale he cannot accept. She came forward from the year 1574 to save Quincy's sister-in-law Loni, who lies dying from leukemia. It seems the only way to break the curse that has plagued the Harrigan women is for Quincy and Ceara to marry. NOW. Against his better judgment, Quincy and Ceara are married. What comes next is a beautiful love story as husband and wife fall in love with one another. Ceara's astonishment at modern amenities such as cell phones, showers, and cars is pure fun to read, and their lovemaking is sexy and hot enough to warm the cold nights on Quincy's ranch.

Coffman, Elaine.
The Return of Black Douglas. Sourcebooks. 2011. ISBN 9781402250743. 448pp.

Instead of traveling through Scotland with her new husband, Isobella is traveling with her twin sister, Elizabeth, after her fiancé called off their wedding. While moping around the tombs of her ancestors and musing about the lack of quality men around today, she and Elizabeth are whisked off the 16th-century Scotland by a mischievous, match-making ghost named the Black Douglas. Immediately upon arriving in the 16th century, Elizabeth is captured by the Macleans. Isobella is rescued by Alysandir Mackinnon, ruler of clan Mackinnon. A no-nonsense leader, he has a soft spot for those in need but he is not entirely sure what to make of this scantily clad female. He is certain she is a spy. Trying to find her sister and adjust to her new surroundings has Isobella feeling more than a bit lost. Alysandir does his best to make her feel welcome while fighting his attraction to her. Isobella fights her attraction as well. She doesn't know if she is going to stay here or go home, and she doesn't want another broken heart. Black Douglas isn't about to let these two get away with ignoring his matchmaking and sets about to make them see how perfect they are for each other. (Mackinnon-Douglas, #2)

Cready, Gwyn. ♈
Seducing Mr. Darcy. 2008. Pocket Books. ISBN 9781416541165. 374pp.

You will never look at a Jane Austen book in the same way again. Flip Allison isn't thrilled when her book club chooses *Pride and Prejudice (P&P)* as their next group read. Where's the sex? Where's the angst? Where's the heat? Ranting against the book in earshot of an Austen expert, Magnus Knightley leads her to indulge in a mood-lifting massage. Her masseuse includes the advice to visualizing herself in her favorite book. *P&P* manages to hijack her sexy daydream, and she finds herself enjoying a fantasy romp with Mr. Darcy himself. Invigorated from the massage and daydream, Flip heads off to book group, where the discussion of *P&P* takes on a decidedly different turn. Somehow Mr. Darcy and Lizzie are arguing over her! Somehow she has changed the book. The only person she can think of to help fix this is the arrogant and too handsome Magnus. He lends more than a helping hand in fixing the problem. A steamy and uproarious addition to the Austen files.

Kurland, Lynn.
Roses in Moonlight. 2013. Jove. ISBN 9780515153460. 353pp.

Twenty-six-year-old textile expert Samantha Drummond is eager to get out from under her overbearing mother's thumb. She finally breaks free by agreeing to housesit for friends in England for the summer. She had no idea that her summer would be spent on strange errands and wild chases. It all started when she was asked to deliver a piece of lace. That piece of lace is highly coveted by Derrick Cameron, time traveler, adventurer, and antique hunter. He will do anything to get it back, including hurling himself and Samantha back in time. Derrick is a well-seasoned time traveler, and he moves seamlessly between centuries. Samantha needs little more help adjusting. Learning to trust one another as they move from one crazy scheme to another opens their eyes to the slowly building attraction between them in this gentle addition to Kurland's series. (De Piaget, #15)

Lamm, Gina.
The Geek Girl and the Scandalous Earl. 2013. Sourcebooks. ISBN 978140 2277597. 352pp.

The only reason Jamie Marten agreed to help haul antiques is because she was getting Comic-Con tickets out of it. What she got was a whole lot more. Jamie is transported 200 years into the past to the home of Micah Axelby, Earl of Dunnington. Micah has been trying to repair his reputation with the ton after a scandal with his mistress. The last thing he needs is another scandal. And Jamie turns out to be one small scandal after another. She has a difficult time adjusting to the mores and rules of 1816 London and is sorely missing hot showers and her online games. Her only consolation is that the earl is very easy on the eyes, and when they aren't bickering like children, he is quite nice to her and she might even like him. Micah has his hands full with an ex-lover and a woman he is planning on proposing to, but there is something about this Jamie with the bird game on her talking box that he can't put out of his mind. A meddlesome housekeeper, a not–so-loyal greyhound named Baron, and a helpful chambermaid round out the cast of this light and fun time travel romance.

Markham, Wendy.
If Only in My Dreams. 2006. Signet. ISBN 9780451220035. 400pp.

This engaging time travel romance begins with actress Clara McCallum set to star in a World War II epic based on a true story. It won't be a very merry Christmas for Clara—due to the movie's schedule; she will be alone in New York City and she has just been diagnosed with breast cancer. While filming, Clara steps off a train into 1941 and meets Jed Landry, the doomed soldier that her character falls in love with in the movie. Clara falls for Jed and is torn between returning to New York for treatments and staying in the past to try to save Jed from his fate. A bittersweet romance with strong characters; readers will be anxious to find out what happens next for Clara in Markham's sequel *The Best Gift*.

Mayhue, Melissa.
Highlanders Curse. 2011. Pocket Star. ISBN 9781439190326. 384pp.
 Archeologist Abigail Porter has a knack for finding things, which makes her very good at what she does. So good that she is offered a spot on a dig in Scotland. In celebration of the good news, Abigail has one too many at girls' night out. She might have wished for the perfect man. She might have had a one-night stand. She's not exactly sure what happened, but she is sure that there is a very hunky, naked man in her bed. The naked man, Colin Macalister, is a medieval Highlander cursed by the Fae Queen and to be banished to the future. Crazy as it sounds, it begins to make sense when suddenly her life is in danger, and at Colin's urging, she uses her newly discovered Fae powers to send them back to his home. There he can keep her safe and give in to the desire that he has felt for her since he woke up next to her. Abby needs to decide where she belongs, here with Colin and her heart or back in the future. (Daughters of the Glen, #8)

Reality TV

Lights, Camera, Action. . . . LOVE! We all know that reality TV is not reality and that events are changed, conversations are taken out of context, and artificial drama is introduced. Can a girl really find true love in this environment, or will love only last as long as the camera is rolling?

Ford, Julie N.
Count Down to Love. 2011. Boneville. ISBN 9781599555164. 234pp.
 Country music singer Kelly Grace Pickens never wanted a big wedding, and when her fiancé/manager Trevor leaves her at the altar, she's not sure what to do. She didn't get the touring gig she was counting on and it seems that Trevor has been pocketing the mortgage payments, so she's not just broke, but homeless, too. Her cousin Sissy is the co-producer of the hit reality show *Count Down to Love*. They are due to start filming in a week, and one of the contestants is no longer available. Kelly agrees to take her place but is sure that she'll be the first to go. Kelly's not looking for love, only the paycheck she'll get for being on the show. However, Kelly is drawn to the show's bachelor, New York millionaire Dillon Black, and he seems to see something in her, too. When Trevor turns up, Kelly has some tough decisions to make, but her faith will help her make the right choice. A fast-paced, fun story with a sweet character who matures and grows as the story progresses.

MacAlister, Katie.
The Corset Diaries. 2004. Onyx. ISBN 9780451411129. 336pp.

After nursing her husband through a long illness, 39-year-old "skinny-challenged" Tessa Riordan is a widow with more medical bills than she knows what to do with, and her job as a historian will never make a dent in what she owes. When a friend calls and offers her a chance to appear in the new British reality show *A Month in the Life of a Victorian Duke,* she jumps at the chance but then worries that her weight will be an issue. Tessa is to play an American duchess opposite Max Edgerton, an incredibly yummy architect, who will be the duke. Life in Victorian times turns out to be harder than you'd think, even for the lady of the manor, and Tessa gets herself into one hysterical situation after another. Despite a really awful first meeting, sparks fly between Tessa and Max, but Tessa's not sure if it is all for show or if it could be something real. Told through a series of diary entries, the story moves quickly with lots of zany characters, crazy situations, and down and dirty sex. If Katie MacAlister doesn't make you laugh, there is something wrong with your funny bone.

Quick, Katherine.
Ineligible Bachelor. 2013. Montlake Romance. ISBN 9781612186863. 181pp.

Frederika "Rikka," not "Freddy" McAllister, has finally come up with a foolproof plan to get lifelong crush Logan Gabriel to notice her as more than just the girl next door. She enters him in *Elan* magazine's *Most Eligible Bachelor* contest, planning to be there to cheer him up when he loses. Unfortunately for Freddy, Logan is chosen to be the star of *Eligible Bachelor,* and she must go along with him to the mansion in New Jersey to eliminate five of the six beautiful contestants, until only his perfect match remains. Logan can't believe that Freddy has done this to him. The only upside is that they'll get to spend more time together. Thoughts like that make him wonder if he's already found his perfect match, but if that were true, she never would have gotten him into this mess, would she? A sassy and sweet contemporary romance with great one-liners, *Ineligible Bachelor* is the first in a planned trilogy.

Sparks, Kerrelyn.
Vamps and the City. 2006. Avon. ISBN 9780060752019. 387pp.

Four years ago, Darcy Newhart almost died; instead, she was turned into a vampire. She hates being a vampire, is bored with being part of a harem, and misses her career in TV. She comes up with an idea for DVN, the Digital Vampire Network, to produce a show called *The Sexiest Man on Earth*." The winner of the show will take over as master of the harem, now that Roman Draganesti (the hero of the first book) is getting married. To create more interest, Darcy is including a few mortals as contestants. One of those mortals, Austin Erickson, is a vampire hunter and member of the CIA's Stake-Out team; he has been tasked with rescuing Shanna Whelan, Roman Draganesti's bride to be. Austin has psychic abilities and can read people's minds.

He quickly falls for Darcy but doubts that she is truly a vampire since her thoughts are never about blood. Darcy finds herself falling for him, too, but can a beautiful vampire and a vampire hunter really find true love and happiness? Sparks' second book in the Love at Stake series brings back many of the characters from the first book, while introducing several new ones. She has created an intriguing vampire world and fills it with laugh-out-loud moments. Readers who are looking for a new twist on vampires will enjoy this entertaining series.

Wardell, Heather.

▶ *Seven Exes Are Eight Too Many*. 2010. Heather Wardell. ISBN 9781452893204. 276pp.

Madeleine-Cora "MC" Spencer had a little too much to drink the night she filled out the application for *Find Your Prince* and has regretted it ever since. After being notified that she is to be a contestant, she studies the show to come up with a strategy for finding love and shops for some cute outfits. She gets the surprise of her life when she realizes the producers have lied to her. For the next 21 days, MC and seven of her ex-boyfriends will be competing against Kent (the one who got away) and seven of his ex-girlfriends for one million dollars. Is it possible to find true love when the only available men are your exes? Wardell has a very unique writing style, combining laugh-until-you-cry humor with intense emotions. The secondary characters are well developed, the story moves quickly, and the background information on reality TV is fascinating.

Williams, Kathryn.

Pizza, Love, and Other Stuff That Made Me Famous. 2012. ISBN 97808050 92851. 240pp. Y A

Sixteen-year-old Sophie Nicolaides works in her family's Greek-Italian restaurant, Taverna Ristorante, but has dreams of someday being a famous chef. When her best friend and crush Alex suggests that she audition for *Teen Test Kitchen,* she isn't too keen on the idea until she learns that the prize includes a scholarship to culinary school. Sophie is selected as a contestant and gets to spend seven weeks in Napa, California, at the culinary school. Once on set, she finds that being on a reality show is nothing like she thought it would be and discovers that she still has a lot to learn about being herself. A light romance develops between Sophie and the dreamy French student Luc but what about Alex? Includes recipes. A light, witty story that's just perfect to curl up with on a rainy Sunday afternoon.

Wingate, Lisa.

Talk of the Town. 2008. Bethany House. ISBN 9780764204906. 368pp.

American Megastar is the hottest reality show on TV. The top finalists have been selected, and it is time for the surprise hometown reunion concerts. The story is told in alternating chapters by Mandalay Florentino, who has been sent to Daily, Texas, for the weekend to prepare for the return of gospel singer Amber Amberson, and Imagene Doll, a recent widow who has lived her whole life in Daily. Mandalay is trying to keep the reason she's in Daily under wraps, but it's hard to keep a secret in a town so small. Mandalay's got the perfect life—an important job in Los Angeles and a fiancé, even if she doesn't have a ring yet. But Carter Woods, the sexy cowboy renting the room next door to Mandalay, seems to show up everywhere Mandalay goes. Maybe God has a different plan in mind for her? Quirky characters and a down-home Texas setting are a big part of this light inspirational romance. (Daily, Texas #1)

Men in Kilts

What's not to love about a man in a kilt?

DeHart, Robyn.
Treasure Me. 2011. Forever. ISBN 9780446541985. 352pp.

If one was two days away from her wedding and found her fiancé in a compromising position with her sister, what would one do? Head to the High-lands to study the Loch Ness monster? Probably not but our heroine, Vanessa Pembrooke, does just that. Traveling solo during Victorian times is disap-proved of and for good reason. After a near miss with a few unruly patrons at a pub, Vanessa finds herself married, handfasted to Graeme Langford, a treasure hunter who came to her rescue. Now the two are running for their lives dodging bullets and villains as they search for Nessie and the Stone of Destiny. Graeme wasn't looking for a bride, and Vanessa wasn't looking for a groom, but along the adventure trail they begin to see each other as husband and wife in more ways than one. (Legend Hunters, #3)

Forester, Amanda.
Highlander's Heart. 2011. Sourcebooks. ISBN 9781402253041. 448pp. (High-lander, #2)

In 14th-century Scotland, having left her abusive husband five years ago and now having no one to protect her since her uncle's death, Lady Isabelle Tyn-sdale knew that she must get to the king to have her marriage annulled. While attempting to get back to court, she is saved from an attack by Laird David Campbell. The laird vows to help Isabelle get to court, even though there is a bounty on his head should he be captured on English soil. Isabelle tries to keep her noble heritage a secret, but once David finds out, he attempts to keep her as a prisoner to ransom back to the court and to pay off his bounty. He didn't plan on falling in love with his prisoner, nor did she plan on falling for her jailer. Vivid attention to details bring the Highlands of Scotland to life but do not intrude on the growing romance between Lady Isabelle and Laird David.

Howell, Hannah.
▶ *Highland Master*. 2013. Zebra. ISBN 9781420118810. 352pp.

In the latest book in the Murray Family series, Lady Triona McKee didn't envision her life turning out this way. Her husband, the laird, had died along with half the men in the clan from illness. Luckily before he died, he left a will naming her as Laird of the McKee clan. However, the men who are left head to France to hire themselves out for coin. Alone and defenseless, Lady Triona is at her wits' end trying to fend off her neighbor who is doing his best to convince her that she needs his protection and hand in marriage. Thankfully, her cousin Adrianna comes to her lands with several of her men to guard Lady Triona. The men immediately take action and set out to thwart her neighbor's advances and his attempts to prove that Lady Triona can't rule the land. One of the guards, the widowed Sir Brett Murray, has sworn off love until he sees Lady Triona. Smitten by her, he might change his mind. He must decide whether or not it is worth the risk of opening his heart again.

Mallory, Margaret.
The Chieftain. 2013. Forever. ISBN 9780446583114. 391pp.

Only 19 and already a widow, Ilyssa, a healer with the gift of second sight, quietly runs the Chieftain Connor's household with authority and gentleness. When Connor comes home from war and moves his household, she moves with him taking her love for him along. Knowing that as chieftain he must marry to create an alliance between his clan and a rival faction, Connor cannot, and does not, waste time thinking about love. So why can't he get sweet Ilyssa out of his mind and thoughts?

McCarty, Monica.
The Hunter. 2013. Ballantine. ISBN 9780345543912. 380pp.

In the Scotish Highlands, an expert tracker and an elite spy trying to outdo one another in war in this historically accurate romance. Ewen Lamont is the hunter who is seeking Lady Janet of Mar he knows her as Sister Genna, an Italian nun with whom he shared a sensual stolen kiss. Both Lady Janet and Ewen are stubborn and devoted to their causes. In spite of this, the buried passion from their stolen kiss takes over and claims them both. (Highland Guard, #7)

McQuinston, Jennifer.
What Happens in Scotland. 2013. Avon. ISBN 9780062231291. 384pp.

Over the course of 24 hours in Scotland, Georgette Thorold and James McKenzie have to work together to figure out what happened last night. Neither is too clear on what happened or how they came to wake together in an inn married to one another. While their memories may not be entirely clear, their attraction to each other is. Was last night a mistake or a happy accident that brought them together as man and wife?

Roberts, Victoria.
Temptation in a Kilt. 2012. Sourcebooks. ISBN 9781402270062. 352pp.

Fleeing an arranged marriage, Rosalia is determined to make it to her ancestral home in Glengarry. Realizing that it is too dangerous to travel unescorted, she allows herself to be taken in by Laird Ciaran MacGregor. While staying with Ciaran, Rosalia's feelings for the laird deepen from friendship to love and his do for her. Their road to happiness is pitted with a jealous mistress and enemy clans to be defeated. A solid gentle Highlander debut. (Bad Boys of the Highlands, #1)

Save a Horse, Ride a Cowboy

Although it's no longer uncharted territory, stories set in the West still seem romantic.

Brown, Carolyn.
I Love This Bar. 2010. Sourcebooks Casablanca. ISBN 9781402239267. 384pp.

Daisy isn't looking for a man in her life or romance, but she literally falls for sexy newcomer Jarrod when they collide on the floor of her bar. The whole county of Erath, Texas, knows that Jarrod is only sticking around long enough to help his cranky uncle get his ranch in shape again. Daisy isn't about to fall for someone who isn't going to be around for the long haul. Still, the two keep running into each other, and Jarrod is going to do his best to prove to Daisy that he belongs in her life and in her bed. (Honky Tonk, #1)

Johnson, Cat.
One Night with a Cowboy. 2013. Brava. ISBN 9780758285386. 287pp.

Dr. Rebecca Hart is not having a good day; her job as an English professor at a prestigious college is downsized, and she gets home just in time to see her boyfriend packing up the last of his things. A New Yorker through and through, she insists that her sister go with her to a job interview in Oklahoma, when Emma sends in an application on her behalf without telling her. After an evening at the rodeo, Becca has a sizzling one-night stand with a hot cowboy. Neither expects to see the other again, but at an Oklahoma State University faculty mixer, Becca, comes face to face with Staff Sergeant Tucker Jenkins from the Reserve Officer's Training Corp program. Neither one is looking for a relationship, but they can't deny the spark between them. Johnson takes a lust-at-first-sight story between two very different characters and turns it into something more. The Oklahoma Nights series continues with *Two Times as Hot* and *Three Weeks with a Bull Rider.*

Kayne, Stacey.
Mustang Wild. 2007. Harlequin. ISBN 9780373294411. 296pp.

Mustanger Skylar Daines is just trying to get to Wyoming from the New Mexican Territory and make a home for herself and her younger brother,

Garrett. Nothing is going to stop her from claiming her father's land, not even her husband. When she ends up accidentally married to incredibly sexy former bounty hunter Tucker Morgan, the only logical thing to do is have the marriage annulled. Even though he is a confirmed bachelor and will tell you that he is a womanizing son of a gun, there is something about Skylar that has him thinking that maybe a home and a family wouldn't be such a bad idea after all. Now the reins are in Skylar's hands. Should she stay or should she go? (Wild, #1)

Kelly, Carla.
Borrowed Light. 2011. Bonneville. ISBN 9781599554662. 410pp.
  After completing a course at the Fannie Farmer School of Cookery in Boston, Julia Darling returns home to Salt Lake City in 1909. Uncertain about her engagement, she decides to call it off when she sees a help-wanted ad for a cook who studied with Fannie Farmer posted by a rancher in Wyoming. Julia realizes that she may be in over her head after arriving at the ranch; the kitchen is a disaster and the ranch hands are not impressed with her fancy cooking. She hears rumors about her boss, Paul Otto, and isn't sure what to believe. Julia also struggles with her faith; she has feelings for Paul but could never marry someone who isn't Mormon. Kelly is well known for her regency romances; this is her first venture into inspirational romance, but according to her website, her future books will have the same focus.

Klein, K.C.
Texas Wide Open. 2012. Kensington Trade. ISBN 9781601831989. 276pp.
  It seems that Kate Harris has loved Cole Logan, her next-door neighbor, her whole life. She thought that they were destined for each other. They would stay on her daddy's ranch and live happily ever after. When Cole didn't return her feelings, she took matters into her own hands and made a pass at him when she was 17. Eight years older than she, Cole turned her down and drove her off. Only a call from Cole telling her that her beloved father is ill brings her home. Having moved on from Cole, Kate is determined to see her father through this illness and go back to her fiancé. That is until she sees Cole again and he still takes her breath away. If she can get over his rejection, maybe her long-awaited dream can come true. (New Adult)

Lindsey, Johanna.
One Heart to Win. 2013. Gallery. ISBN 9781476714301. 384pp.
  How far would you go to put a stop to a family feud? Travel from Boston to Montana? Tiffany is trying to do the right thing and doing what her mother asks, so she not only travels across the country but also agrees to marry a man she has never met in hopes of stopping a longstanding family feud. Her careful plans go out the window when the train she is riding is robbed and, in the midst of the confusion, her identity is switched. Suddenly Tiffany, the bride-to-be is Jennifer, the housekeeper. One more snafu lands Jennifer in the home of her

would-be fiancé, where she finds that for the enemy, he isn't so bad. Her feelings grow for Hunter, but what will happen when he finds out the truth? A light and, often funny, case of looking for love in all the wrong places.

Miller, Linda Lael.
Big Sky Country. 2012. Harlequin. ISBN 9780373776436. 384pp.

Joslyn Kirk is returning home to Parable, Montana, to the only place she ever called home. Trying to create a life for herself, she reconnects with Kendra, her old high school friend, who gives her a job and a place to live. In Parable, Slade Barlow is now sheriff, but back then he was just the poor, illegitimate son of one of the county's wealthy ranchers with an unrequited crush on Joslyn. Joslyn and Kendra, along with Slade's half brother Hutch, weren't too nice to Slade as kids, but times change and so do people. At least that is what Joslyn wants to think. As she and the very sexy Slade keep running into each other, she is more than willing to give the good sheriff another chance at winning her heart. First in the Parable Montana series.

Warner, Kaki. ♟
▶ *Pieces of Sky*. 2010. Berkley. ISBN 9780425232149. 432pp.

Fleeing her home in England after being raped by her sister's husband, Jessica Thornton is traveling to the New Mexico Territory in 1869, where she hopes to find her brother. Nothing in her privileged upbringing has prepared her for the difficult journey or the unrelenting heat. A stagecoach accident forces her to take shelter at Brady Wilkins's ranch. Jessica and Brady are drawn to each other, but they are opposites in so many ways—Jessica is a British heiress who writes pamphlets on proper etiquette, and Brady never learned how a gentleman should behave. Jessica is still in danger of losing her estate in Northumberland, and Brady and his two brothers are fighting a family feud with the son of Rosa Roja's previous owner. Warner's does not gloss over the conditions of the West during this time period; people and animals die, and life is hard. Her characters grow to love each other slowly, and the time allowed makes their romance all the more satisfying for the reader. (Blood Rose trilogy, #1)

Rx for Love

Tensions run high in hospitals and medical situations, but so do emotions.

Andre, Bella.
Love Me. 2010. Createspace. ISBN 9781453669976. 218pp.

When you have been in love with someone from afar for what seems like forever and he shows up on your doorstep looking incredibly sexy, what do you do? If you are Janica and he is emergency room doctor Luke who happens to also be your brother-in-law, you try to fight it. Until you don't and you end up having the best one-night stand of your life. Then you put it out of your head. Until you don't and you can't stop thinking about him. Luke doesn't realize the depth of his own feelings until it looks like Janica might not be there for him. (Take Me, #2)

Calvert, Candace.
Critical Care. 2009. Tyndale House. ISBN 978141325439. 304pp.
   Claire hasn't stepped foot in an emergency room (since the awful day her brother Kevin died. Now the hospital, where she is working in Nursing Education, she is faced with a disaster and is called upon to put the Crisis Management plan into place. It might not be so bad if the ER director didn't think that counseling was a bunch of touchy feely nonsense or if she wasn't madly attracted to him. With the help of her new friends at the ER and God's presence, she is able to deal with the aftermath of her own tragedy and to find a new love with Dr. Caldwell. Dr. Caldwell faces his own demons and comes to terms with them, letting first God into his heart and then Claire. (Mercy Hospital, #1)

Fox, Angie.
Immortally Yours. 2012. St. Martins. ISBN 9780312546663. 306pp.
   "Incoming Wounded" takes on a different meaning when you are literally in limbo between worlds and patching up wounded gods, vampires, werewolves, and other creatures. Dr. Petra Robichaud is thrust into the strange world of the M.A.S.H. 3063 when she is drafted from her sleepy supernatural clinic in New Orleans to the Limbo lands. Things take a turn when Galen, a Greek demigod, lands on her operating table and sets not only an ancient prophecy into motion but also her emotions reeling. Can she save him, the world, and her heart? (Monster M.A.S.H., #1)

Ione, Larissa.
Pleasure Unbound. 2008. Forever. ISBN 9780446401036. 389pp.
   If you are a hurt demon, you head to UGH—The Underground General Hospital where Eidolon, the best demon doctor around, practices. If you are a demon slayer, you try to steer clear of the place unless you are hurt so badly that you tag along for the ride with your intended victim. Tayla, the demon slayer, falls hard for Eidolon who also happens to be an incubus demon. While being treated by, and having sex with, the demon doctor, it is revealed that Tayla is part demon herself. As she comes to terms with this news, she is forced to choose between her coworkers and her new lover. For Eidolon's part, he must determine where his loyalties lie as well, with his fellow demons or with the woman who sets his soul afire. First in the Demonica series.

McCarthy, Erin.
▶ *Houston, We Have Problem*. 2004. Brava. ISBN 9780758205971. 293pp.
   For resident Josie Adkins, her rotation in orthopedics at a small hospital in Florida was supposed to be a cinch. It was until the very sexy, very out of her

league Dr. Houston Hayes turned up as her attending physician. Bad enough he is drop-dead gorgeous and a top-notch surgeon, he also has an ego to match it. Whenever Josie is around him, she turns into a first-class klutz. For his part, Dr. Hayes can't believe how Josie is getting to him. He's never felt this way about a woman, but he isn't about to let her know that he wants her body and soul. For now, he has a bold and very unorthodox offer of one night of wild, no-strings-attached sex. Josie wants more but is willing to take a chance on the good doctor.

McCoy, Judi.
One Night with a Goddess. 2007. Avon. ISBN 9780060774608. 384pp.

When your Dad is Zeus and he issues a punishment, you know it is going to be a doozy. For Chole, the Muse of Happiness, her punishment is spending a year as a mortal. Of course, there is a catch. Date all you want, says Zeus, but don't fall in love with a mortal. She can do that; with her flair for passion and fashion, she is sure that the year will pass quickly and soon enough she will be back home on Mount Olympus living the luxurious immortal life she knows she was born to live. Chloe lands a job as an assistant wedding planner with the sweet Isabelle Castleberry. All is going fine until the very handsome, very sexy Dr. Matthew Castleberry arrives to spend time with his grandmother and recover from his stint with Doctors without Borders. Attracted to the sexy doctor but knowing her time in the mortal world is almost up, Chloe isn't sure what to do. Zeus and Eros as well as other Greek gods make appearances throughout the novel. Luckily, the good doctor knows exactly what Chloe needs in this fun breezy romance. (Goddess, #2)

Ortolon, Julie.
Just Perfect. 2005. Signet. ISBN 9780451216885. 304pp.

Dr. Christine Ashton is a no-nonsense ER doc who isn't afraid of anything, except heights, which puts a damper on her love for skiing. Using her no-nonsense ER doc approach, she embarks on a ski trip determined to conquer this fear. That might be easier than keeping away from the hunky ski instructor, Alec. He's just the type she is trying to avoid. The gorgeous, go-nowhere ski bum type. Then disaster strikes, throwing them together in a situation that reveals he is more than just a ski bum and maybe, just maybe, he is exactly the right type for her.

Appendix: RITA Award Winners, 2007–2013

Best Contemporary Single-Title Romance

2013   *The Way Back Home* by Barbara Freethy
2012   *Boomerang Bride* by Fiona Lowe
2011   *Simply Irresistible* by Jill Shalvis
2010   *Too Good to Be True* by Kristan Higgins
2009   *Not Another Bad Date* by Rachel Gibson
2008   *Catch of the Day* by Kristan Higgins
2007   *Adios to My Old Life* by Caridad Ferrer

Best First Book

2013   *The Haunting of Maddy Clare* by Simone St. James
2012   *First Grave on the Right* by Darynda Jones
2011   *Pieces of Sky* by Kaki Warner
2010   *One Scream Away* by Kate Brady
2009   *Oh. My. Gods.* By Tera Lynn Childs
2008   *Dead Girls Are Easy* by Terri Garey
2007   *The Husband Trap* by Tracy Anne Warren

Best Historical Romance

2013   *A Rogue by Any Other Name* by Sarah MacLean
2012   *The Black Hawk* by Joanna Bourne
2011   *His at Night* by Sherry Thomas
2010   *Not Quite a Husband* by Sherry Thomas

125

2009   *The Edge of Impropriety* by Pam Rosenthal
2008   *Lessons of Desire* by Madeline Hunter
2007   (No Award Given)

Best Inspirational

2013   *Against the Tide* by Elizabeth Camden
2012   *The Measure of Katie Calloway* by Serena Miller
2011   *In Harm's Way* by Irene Hannon
2010   *The Inheritance* by Tamera Alexander
2009   *Finding Stefanie* by Susan May Warren
2008   *A Touch of Grace* by Linda Goodnight
2007   *Revealed* by Tamera Alexander

Best Paranormal

2013   *Shadow's Claim* by Kresley Cole
2012   *Dragon Bound* by Thea Harrison
2011   *Unchained* by Sharon Ashwood
2010   *Kiss of a Demon King* by Kresley Cole
2009   *Seducing Mr. Darcy* by Gwyn Cready
2008   *Lover Revealed* by J.R. Ward
2007   *A Hunger like No Other* by Kresley Cole

Best Regency

2013   (No Award Given)
2012   *A Night to Surrender* by Tessa Dare
2011   *The Mischief of the Mistletoe* by Lauren Willig
2010   *What Happens in London* by Julia Quinn
2009   *My Lord and Spymaster* by Joanna Bourne
2008   *The Secret Diaries of Miss Miranda Cheever* by Julia Quinn
2007   (No Award Given)

Best Romance Novella

2013   *Seduced by a Pirate* by Eloisa James
2012   *I Love the Earl* by Caroline Linden
2011   "Shifting Sea" by Virginia Kantra in *Burning Up*
2010   "The Christmas Eve Promise" by Molly O'Keefe in *The Night before Christmas*
2009   "The Fall of Rogue Gerard" by Stephanie Laurens in *It Happened One Night*

2008 "Born in My Heart" by Jennifer Greene in *Like Mother, like Daughter*
2007 "Tis the Silly Season" in *A NASCAR Holiday* by Roxanne St. Claire

Best Romantic Suspense

2013 *Scorched* by Laura Griffin
2012 *New York to Dallas* by J. D. Robb
2011 *Silent Scream* by Karen Rose
2010 *Whisper of Warning* by Laura Griffin
2009 *Take No Prisoners* by Cindy Gerard
2008 *Ice Blue* by Anne Stuart
2007 *Blackout* by Annie Solomon

Best Young Adult Romance

2013 *The Farm* by Emily McKay
2012 *Enclave* by Ann Aguirre
2011 *The Iron King* by Julie Kagawa
2010 *Perfect Chemistry* by Simone Elkeles
2009 *Hell Week* by Rosemary Clement-Moore
2008 *Wicked Lovely* by Melissa Marr
2007 (No Award Given)

Index

About the Authors

C. L. QUILLEN is the supervising librarian at the West Caldwell Library, New Jersey. She has presented on a variety of different readers' advisory topics, including mystery, romance, and women's fiction. Quillen is a founding member of the New Jersey Library Association's Readers' Advisory Roundtable, on which she has served as both the chair and vice chair. She received her master's degree from the University of North Carolina at Chapel Hill.

ILENE N. LEFKOWITZ is the supervising librarian of adult services at the Denville Public Library, New Jersey. She has been an active participant in the New Jersey Library Association Readers' Advisory Roundtable for the past 10 years, formerly serving as both the chair and vice chair. She holds a master's degree in library science from Rutgers University.